The Lion Inside

A Girl's Guide On How To Get What
They Want And Live An Abundant Life.

By

Robert N. Jacobs

Grosvenor House
Publishing Limited

The right of Robert N. Jacobs to be identified as the author of this
work has been asserted in accordance with Section 78
of the Copyright, Designs and Patents Act 1988

The book cover is copyright to Robert N. Jacobs

This book is published by
Grosvenor House Publishing Ltd
Link House
140 The Broadway, Tolworth, Surrey, KT6 7HT.
www.grosvenorhousepublishing.co.uk

A CIP record for this book
is available from the British Library

ISBN 978-1-80381-359-2

Acknowledgments

"I really mostly just want to thank my beautiful wife, Simona. She was the one who had to put up with me while writing this book. That she did so with love and patience and encouragement instead of strangling me and hiding my body, and then pretending she had never been married to me at all is a testament to the fact that she is, in fact, the single best person I know. I love her more than I can actually express in words – an irony for a writer – and am every day genuinely amazed I get to spend my life with her. You have this book because of her."

To Ava

"Always remember, you have within you the strength, courage, curiosity and the tenacity to follow your passions and reach the stars to change the world. This book is for you."

Foreword

In the developed Western world, there's probably never been a better time to be young. Potentially. There's no shortage of people alive today (in fact, I'm one of them) who can remember when, except for the favoured few born with a silver spoon who could make their own decisions, most people's lives were mapped out for them. The young men and young women in whole villages knew exactly what they were going to do with the rest of their lives (and it wouldn't be the same thing – girls and boys were subject to different expectations). Even in towns and cities of reasonable size, the options were few – I grew up in a city of 350,000 and I knew from childhood that, as a boy, I would be a welder or a fitter, join the armed services or be a copper or a clerk. (As it happens, I dodged the bullet – but to do it I had to travel more than 4,000 miles to a place I'd never seen before and could hardly find on a map.)

Life today isn't like that. All those clerical jobs are gone and the factories and shipyards where I was raised have closed. But new opportunities have arisen in their place. Better opportunities. My grandchildren may end up doing things I didn't dare dream of. The world is their oyster. But only if they let it – and since my grandchildren are girls, that's even more true for them than it would have been if they were boys.

What can hold them back? Themselves – they can hold themselves back. This world of immense opportunity for all is so new that most people (once again, apart from the favoured few whose exclusive schools are there to make sure they don't miss the point) aren't yet quite tuned in to it. They hear negative input – teachers tell them they'll never achieve what they aspire to, well-meaning parents tell them not to set their sights too high for fear of disappointment, and the neighbours say, 'It's a lovely idea, but it isn't for people like us. People from around here don't do that sort of thing.'

If you know a young person whose hearing that sort of negativity right now, buy them this book. If you are one of those young people, buy it yourself. And READ it. Because Robert Jacobs has put together a guidebook to show you, step-by-step, how to get to the place you want to reach. He knows that, today, the world is so full of opportunities that you can achieve anything you set your heart on. If you want it enough, and if you're prepared to go after it, guns blazing.

That doesn't mean this book will tell you how to become a millionaire entrepreneur if that's not what, deep down, you have inside you and what you want. It won't help you become Prime Minister of the UK or President of the United States, either. What it offers is something far better. It shows you how to be the very best YOU possibly can be. And nothing on earth is capable of giving you greater pleasure than that.

You have been born into a world of immense possibilities. You can achieve anything you set your mind to. As long as you really want to. And the messages in this book are far more important if you're a girl than if you're a boy. Because, however great the progress may have been in winning equality between the sexes, there are still more constraints on the progress girls can make than there are on boys. But those constraints only work if you listen to them. Someone may tell you that the job you want is not really a job for girls. The number of people telling you that may be large enough so that you think they must be right. And, if you think they must be right, then right they will be. But if you tell yourself that these people really don't know what they're talking about – that the world has developed and left them behind – that opportunities today really are as open to girls as to boys – then they will be wrong. And you will be the one who proves it.

Start today. Turn to the first page of Chapter 1 and start reading. There – you're on your way. And nothing is going to stop you.

John Lynch
Father, Author, Humanitarian

Contents

Chapter 1

The Lion Inside

There's a moment in most people's lives – perhaps everyone's – when something happens that reveals the real you. Think of it as what scriptwriters call the inciting event. Every movie you've ever seen and ever will see contains an inciting event. It doesn't come right at the beginning – usually, it happens round about page 10 of the script which means ten minutes after the movie starts, and it is the hook on which the whole movie Is hung. What's interesting about inciting events is that they don't need to be major. It *is* a big event in the movie, *Jaws*, where the inciting event is the death of Chrissie Watkins in a shark attack; in *Glengarry Glen Ross*, on the other hand, it's something as small as an encouraging talk a manager gives to his salesforce. In the same way, the inciting incident in a person's life might be catastrophic or some hardly noticeable incident – what matters is that it leads to the discovery of an inner strength and resilience that was hidden deep within. It's in these moments that you realise your true self and recognise that you already have all the resources you need within you to become the best you can be.

There's an old fable about a lion cub that makes this point beautifully...

One day, a lion cub was playing in the forest while his mother took a nap. Interesting things soon attracted his attention and before long he'd wandered deep into the forest to explore the world beyond his den. There was so much to see that he forgot all about finding his way home, until he realised he was lost. Suddenly frightened, he called out for his mother, frantically running in all directions in the hope of seeing her, but no response came. He was lost and alone.

Tired and weary, the little lion cub had all but given up when a sheep that had recently had its lamb taken away heard his cries. Taking pity on him, she approached and comforted him, and became the cub's adoptive mother. She grew very fond of her foundling, but the cub very quickly grew in size, so much so that there were times when she was almost fearful of him. He often had a far-off look in his eyes that she could never quite understand, but the pair lived happily together as mother and son.

Then, one day, a magnificent lion appeared on the horizon. Standing proud, silhouetted against the sky, he shook his huge mane and roared from his vantage point on the top of a hill. The mighty roar echoed through the hills, leaving the mother sheep trembling with fear, but the lion cub found himself spellbound by the strange sound; a sound that sparked a feeling in him he hadn't experienced before. The lion's roar had touched a chord in his nature and aroused a force within him that brought a strange new consciousness of power – a whole new desire. Instinctively, without any conscious thought, he answered the lion's call with a roar of his own. Trembling with a mix of fear and surprise, the bewildered cub felt suddenly awakened. With only a glance toward his foster mother, he leapt away in the direction of the lion on the hill. The lost lion had found himself.

Until that roar, the cub had gambolled around his sheep mother believing himself to be a lamb, never for one moment imagining he'd become anything else or do anything more than his sheep companions. He never dreamed of having a power within him that could strike terror into other beasts; he simply thought he was a sheep. Like the other sheep, he would run at the sight of a dog and tremble in fear at the sound of a howling wolf. In discovering himself to be a lion, he was amazed to see the creatures he'd feared now fearing him. For as long as he'd believed himself to be one, he had been as timid and retiring as a sheep.

Thinking of himself as a sheep, he had no more strength or courage than an ordinary sheep, and if it had been suggested to him that he had the strength of a lion he would not have believed it, believing himself to be no different from any other of his kind. But, when the lion within him was awakened, he instantly became a new creature; king of his domain with very few beasts to rival him. This awakening unlocked the cub's conscious power, a power he may never have realised had he not heard the lion's roar. The roar from the hilltop had not added anything to his strength, or given him a new power, it had merely unlocked what was already there within him. Of course, after such a startling discovery, this young lion could never again be content to live the life of a sheep. The life of a lion, the liberty of a lion, and the power of a lion was now his.

Why does this story matter? It matters because there's a sleeping lion within all of us. We all have within us the power we need to succeed in life; it's just a question of reaching deep inside and awakening it. Just as the young lion could no longer be satisfied with the life of a sheep once the lion within was awakened, we, as people, can no longer be satisfied with an ordinary life when we realise that we have all we need to live an extraordinary life.

You Are Not a Sheep

Why live half a life when you can live a full life? Why follow the path through life that someone else chooses for you when you can choose your own path? And why limit your achievements to those others believe you are capable of? The world is full of stories about people who have made a great success of their lives even though teachers, relatives and others had told them they would never amount to anything. Robert Browning knew this when he wrote:

> *"Ah, but a man's reach should exceed his grasp,
> Or what's a heaven for?"*

Society has a way of setting false restrictions, for example by creating glass ceilings in the workplace, and promoting certain expectations. This affects all of us, men and women, but it's particularly true in relation to how society sees a woman's place in life. Even in today's world, outdated beliefs still exist about gender roles, and it's easy – in fact, it's natural – to absorb those beliefs and subconsciously take them on as your own. In effect, if you're shown or told often enough that you're a sheep, you begin to believe that you can only ever do what sheep do. Don't let people do that to you. Set your own limits, and keep resetting as you aspire to be all you can be.

Think of all the people that have grown up in impoverished circumstances believing themselves to be no different from those around them, and therefore destined to live a life of poverty. The way they think becomes their reality, but then something happens – that moment of awakening. It may be an emergency, a catastrophic event, an encounter with another individual, or some other challenging experience but, in facing it, they discover the 'inner lion' and inner power they didn't know they had. Through this discovery, they realise that they are not destined to be the same as those around them. Instead, they have what they need to be more: they have all they need to live the life they want.

What makes the difference is self-belief. If you believe you are a sheep, you will go through life following the path of all the sheep that have gone before you. All right, perhaps that's enough talk about sheep because none of us really believes that a sheep is what we are. But the idea remains: until you believe you can be more than you are, you won't be. If the life you currently have is not what you want, you have the power within you to change it – but you must *believe* that change is possible. You can choose to take a different path. And it really is a matter of choice – it's up to you.

That is not to say it's easy. There are lots of examples of people throughout history who would not have believed the things they would go on to achieve in life if they'd been told they would in their childhood. The path you'll take in life is not always clearly defined from a young age, and it's fair to say that many young adults will embark on the career path they think is right for them, only to discover further down the line that it isn't providing the fulfilment they'd hoped for. When that happens, it takes self-belief to change direction and try a different path but when you do so you are choosing not to settle for a half-life. Instead, you are choosing to be and do more. You have made a conscious decision to realise your true potential.

You Are Not Alone

It really is your life to live and your success to achieve, but no one makes it to the top on their own. As humans, we're all connected; everything we do, say, think, and believe has an effect on others. In the grand scale of things, we're all just a part of something much bigger than ourselves. For some, the something bigger is a higher power found in their religious or spiritual beliefs, for others it might be the strength found in being a part of a team with genuine team spirit. Even those who choose to go it alone are connected to others who have followed a similar path before them, and it's in these connections that inspiration is found.

"If I have seen further, it is by standing on the shoulders of giants." – Isaac Newton

Many children grow up wanting to be just like the people they know and admire, whether that's their parents, aunts and uncles, or people they encounter in daily life such as teachers, bus drivers, and shopkeepers. These are people in roles they're familiar with, but it's not unusual for children also to imagine themselves growing up to become a storybook character, a superhero, or some other being who doesn't actually exist. Children don't get hung up on practicalities or realities, they simply use their imagination and dream of being whatever they want. For them, nothing is impossible.

As we grow into teenage years and adulthood, life has a way of taking away the ability to imagine ourselves being whoever and whatever we want to be. Sometimes the negative influence of others around us is responsible. You might have your dreams for your future shot down by someone saying, *"Dream on! You need to get your head out of the clouds and get real,"* or little nagging doubts put into your mind by those around you saying, *"Things like that don't happen to the likes of us."* Over time, the beliefs of others can subconsciously become your own... you believe yourself to be no different from the others around you. The secret is to surround yourself with positive, like-minded people who will not only inspire you to achieve more but will support you in all you do, helping you to wake your inner lion.

Ask yourself, are the things you believe to be impossible *actually* impossible, or are they simply not possible *yet*? Before Neil Armstrong took his "one small step" in 1969, how many people would have believed it was possible to walk on the moon? In more recent history, consider the idea of having 3-D printing machines in our homes and medical specialists being able to print out prosthetic limbs and body parts for use in surgical procedures. Not so many years ago, how many people would have believed this to be impossible? What about the capabilities of the latest smartphones? At the end of the 1960s, IBM would have charged you £500,000 – half a million pounds – for a mainframe that didn't have anything like the power or the capability of a phone you can buy today for a couple of hundred pounds – and you'd have needed a very large room with air conditioning and a false floor to keep it in. Try carrying that around with you. You don't need to go back many years to find a time when few people would have believed that this type of technology would be available to all of us and not just to James Bond.

If no one had believed these things were possible, they would never have happened. The inspired thinkers and doers behind these happenings *made* it possible, and in so doing they made it possible for others to believe in greater possibilities. To get what you want in life, you must believe it's possible for you – that's YOU – to achieve it. Entrepreneur Sir Richard Branson's backstory is a good example. In his teenage years, he wanted to be a magazine editor but with dyslexia, a poor academic history and no relevant experience, no magazine would employ him. He could have chosen to give up on his dream; instead, he chose to establish and publish his own magazine, giving himself the position of editor. From those early beginnings, Richard Branson became an internationally recognised billionaire business magnate. To all intents and purposes, he's a self-made man, but it's important to recognise that he didn't get there on his own. From an early age, he had the support of his parents in all his endeavours – even those that failed – and as an entrepreneur herself, his mother undoubtedly provided an inspirational influence. When asked about his decisions to start new ventures, his airline in particular, he has said, *"My interest in life comes from setting myself huge, apparently unachievable challenges and trying to rise above them... from the perspective of wanting to live life to the full, I felt that I had to attempt it."*

'Trying to rise above...' is an inspirational way of thinking about striving to become more. Sir Richard recognises that, no matter where he is in life, he has the potential to be and do more. As soon as one seemingly impossible goal is achieved, he moves on to the next, highlighting his belief that living life to the full means constantly pushing the limits of what he can achieve. For him, there's no end goal, there's only the *next* goal, and settling for where he is isn't an option when there's a world of possibilities yet to be discovered and explored. Until boundaries are pushed, it's not possible to know what you're capable of, and in Sir Richard's book, *not* attempting new things and challenging yourself to become more equates to living half a life.

"It is the man you are capable of making, not the man you have become, that is most important to you."
– Orison Swett Marsden

Author Orison Swett Marsden wrote those words in the early 1900s, but they still have value today. He likens not challenging ourselves or aspiring to achieve our true potential to being a businessperson with a stack of cash sitting idle in a bank gaining no interest. Just as, in business, money is invested with a view to financial growth, not investing in our own growth is effectively squandering our assets. Aspiring to become your best self is choosing to invest in yourself and to keep growing; it's believing in yourself as the person you aspire to be and choosing to see yourself as that person in the making. As Marsden puts it: *"Try to bring out that possible man... You have assets within you infinitely more valuable than money capital... why not plan to bring out this enormous residue, these great unused resources, this locked-up ability which has never come out of you? You know it is there. You instinctively feel it. Your intuition, your instinct, your ambition tell you that there is a much bigger man in you than you have ever found or used. Why don't you use him, why don't you get at him, why don't you call him out, why don't you stir him up?"*

'Stirring him up' describes Sir Richard Branson's approach to life perfectly. Through his endeavours – successful and otherwise – he not only pushes his own limits; he inspires others to push theirs. He has chosen to dream big dreams and then set about making them his reality, like many inspirational dreamers before him.

Harriet Tubman, an escaped slave who led dozens of slaves to freedom before the Civil War, is an internationally recognised icon of American history. Through her life and legacy, she has inspired countless others from every race and background and once said, *"Every great dream begins with a dreamer. Always remember, you have within you the strength, the patience, and the passion to reach for the stars to change the world."* Born into slavery, Harriet was rented out at the age of just five to work as a nursemaid. Her task was to rock the baby in its cradle, a task that left her with physical and emotional scars as she was whipped whenever the baby cried. At the age of seven, she was rented out to set traps for muskrats, and then to work as a field hand when she became older. Outdoor work was harsh, but in later years she would say that she preferred the physical plantation work to her experience of domestic chores indoors.

By the age of 12, Harriet's dream of justice for all was becoming clear. An overseer on the plantation was about to throw a heavy weight at a slave when she stepped in between them to block the object's path. The weight struck her on her head, leaving her with headaches and narcolepsy for the rest of her life. Poor health and falling asleep at random made her less attractive to slave renters and buyers, meaning she faced even harsher conditions. Around 1840, Harriet's father was given his freedom by his owner, and she discovered that her mother's owner had set her and her children (including Harriet) free in his last will. However, their new owner refused to recognise the will and they were kept in slavery. When it transpired that two of her brothers were about to be sold, Harriet began to plan an escape for all three of them. Some years later, they made their escape, but the brothers decided to turn back. Harriet kept going, and with the help of the Underground Railroad (a network of people offering shelter and aid to enslaved people escaping from the South) she made it to the North and freedom.

Her story could have ended there, but Harriet had a big dream that she wanted to make a reality. Despite having a bounty on her head, she returned south and continued to work as a 'conductor' on the Underground Railway. It wasn't enough that she'd escaped from slavery herself; she wanted to free family, friends, and as many people as possible from enslavement. Her role was made all the more treacherous by the passing of the Fugitive Slave Act in 1850. Freed workers and fugitives in the North could now be captured and returned to slavery, so Harriet's escapees had to be taken even further north to Canada, a task that generally involved travelling at night and carrying a gun for her own protection. Her remarkable skill led to her being known as 'Moses' and, as the years passed, it's reported that Harriet led over 300 enslaved people to freedom though biographers may have exaggerated this number. Harriet never sought glory, but she did take pride in her efforts, once saying, *"I never ran my train off the track, and I never lost a passenger."*

In 1861, the Civil War broke out and Harriet worked as a nurse, cook, and laundress at Fort Monroe, using her knowledge of herbal medicines to do help sick and injured soldiers and fugitives. By 1863, she was a spy for the Union Army, providing crucial intelligence on the whereabouts of Confederate Army soldiers and supplies. After the war, Harriet married and settled with family and friends on land she owned, but she continued to help others by selling homegrown produce, farming pigs, and touring to speak on behalf of the women's suffrage movement. Her dream of change drove her to fight the institution of slavery in extraordinary ways, and her *passion to reach for the stars to change the world* never left her. Harriet died in 1913, but her legacy lives on in the schools and museums that bear her name.

Fast-forward to the 1920s and first lady Eleanor Roosevelt was doing all she could to continue Harriet's dream of racial and social equality. She once said, *"The future belongs to those who believe in the beauty of their dreams."* These women in history dreamt dreams that seemed impossible, but they were not afraid to stir up the bigger person inside them and to live up to those beautiful dreams. When Eleanor became first lady in 1933 she was expected to conform to the traditional role of social hostess, but she chose to challenge the norm and bring about sweeping changes.

Her autonomy was hard-won, and she was reluctant to give up involvement with organisations and causes she felt passionate about. Instead of changing who she was to fit in with expectations, she changed what was expected of a first lady. Having volunteered with the American Red Cross and in Navy hospitals during World War I, been actively involved in the Women's Union Trade League and the League of Women Voters, and been a teacher of American history and literature at a girls' school, as well as raising six children, Eleanor was not prepared to sit back and adopt the role of smiling hostess. Instead, she became and remained a champion of civil rights for African Americans, as well as an advocate for American workers, the poor, young people and women during the Great Depression which began in 1929.

Harriet Tubman and Eleanor Roosevelt came from very different backgrounds, but they had in common a desire to see a better, fairer world for all. Eleanor inspired many women to challenge the norms of the times and to be who they wanted to be. She believed passionately in her causes, and she had courage in her convictions. Never afraid to stir things up and to stand up for her beliefs, she once said, *"Remember always that you have not only the right to be an individual, you have an obligation to be one. You cannot make any useful contribution in life unless you do this."*

Knowing What You Want

When you know what you want, you're already taking a step towards achieving it – mentally. The word 'want' adds power to your thoughts and actions, compared to thinking that achieving something might be a 'nice idea' someday while really not being convinced it will ever happen. Achieving what you want takes commitment and dedicated effort, and it's always going to be easier to do what you *want* to do than something you feel you *have* to do, or *should* be doing.

Not everyone knows what they want from a young age, but something shared by all successful people is always wanting to be the best they can be. For example, when the Beatles were writing songs, they weren't intent on achieving a string of number one hits, they were simply focused on writing the best songs they could – one song at a time. Olympic medallists aspire to win gold, but they succeed by focusing on one training session at a time and always giving their best effort.

Everyone has the capacity to be the best they can be, and your circumstances do not dictate who you are or who you can become. You may not set out in life knowing exactly what career path you want to follow, but you *can* set out knowing the person you want to be. When you know that you want to be the best version of you it's possible to be, you're on your way to realising your true potential – no matter where your journey begins. Those who succeed know that success is a journey, not a destination. Not achieving 'instant' success doesn't mean you can't succeed, and failure to achieve something doesn't make *you* a failure. Your journey to success begins with your decision to succeed. Continuing on your journey takes commitment – the *want* to succeed.

Something it's important to question is whether the dream you're pursuing is *your* dream or the dream someone else has for you. When your dream is in fact someone else's dream for you, you're in danger of doing what you feel you *should* want to do, not what you truly want to do. 'Want' is a word that has power, but when it becomes 'should want', its power is diluted.

Successful people do what they love and love what they do. What you love to do may not be what others believe you should do, but if you're doing what you love, you're going to be doing it often, and through doing – and doing your best – you are going to get better and better at it. You may not have all the external resources you need to succeed initially, but when you have the *want* to succeed, you have all the inner resources you need to bring the people, the things, and the opportunities you need into your life.

Believing in You

Knowing who you want to be, not who others believe you to be, is essential if you are to become that person. The negative voices of doubt can come from many directions, both external and internal, but Vincent Van Gogh once said, *"If you hear a voice within you say, 'You cannot paint,' then by all means paint, and that voice will be silenced."*

To further illustrate this point, here's some food for thought:

- Elvis Presley was turned away by the manager of the Grand Ole Opry. He told him, *"You ain't goin' nowhere, son. You ought to go back to drivin' a truck."*
- Charles Darwin's father told him, *"You will amount to nothing and be a disgrace to your family and yourself."*
- Michael Jordan was initially prevented from joining his high school basketball team because he wasn't tall enough. On his second attempt, he

was cut from the team because the coach didn't think he could play well enough.

- Thomas Edison was informed by a teacher at school that he was, *"too stupid to learn anything."*
- Walt Disney was fired from his newspaper writing job by a boss who told him he, *"lacked imagination."*

Imagine if all these famous people had chosen to adopt the negative opinions of those who didn't believe in them! Instead, they chose to believe in themselves and to continue pursuing their own dreams. They chose to follow their own path and to become the person they knew themselves to be. They recognised their inner lion.

Chapter 2

How to Get What You Want

Successful people are those who believe in their ability to succeed; they believe in themselves. Whatever the goal and however big or small it is, those who achieve are those who believe. No matter how distant it may seem when they set out to achieve it, they *believe* it's possible for them to get the outcome they want. So, the question you now need to answer is, "How strongly do you believe you can have what you want?"

You Are as You Think You Are

The way you think impacts on *everything* you experience in life. Your thoughts influence the way you feel, and those feelings influence the way you perceive reality, or what you believe to be true. What you believe influences the way you feel about things, and those feelings influence the thoughts in your mind... and so the cycle continues. Think of a time when you felt really bored. If your thoughts are all linked to being bored, you're *thinking* about how bored you are, generating *feelings* of boredom, leading to total boredom becoming your perceived reality. You *think* you're bored; therefore you *are* bored. When you realise this, it becomes clear that getting what you want begins and ends with believing that you can.

Everything in the universe is a form of energy, and that includes thoughts and feelings. Everyone is familiar with physical vibrations, but mental vibrations are just as real. Thoughts and emotions are energy, and every thought and feeling creates its own unique vibration. If you try, I'm sure you can remember a time when you walked into a room and felt an 'atmosphere'. What you felt was the energy created by the thoughts and emotions of the people in the room. Those people may not have said a word or even appeared to move, but the vibe you felt (and may have been good but it may also have been bad) was their mental energy.

A 'good' or a 'bad' atmosphere is created by the mental vibrations of others, but it's your own mental energy that's at work when you get a 'good' or a 'bad' feeling about something. You might consider it a gut feeling; that moment when you feel in your gut whether the thing you're about to do is going to be the 'right' or 'wrong' thing for you to do at that time. Energy is all around you, and when you're getting a good feeling about something it's because you're choosing to think positively about it. Your positive thoughts are being sent out into the universe, and the positive energy attracts positive outcomes in return. Of course, if you're getting a bad feeling about something, it's because you're thinking negatively about it. You are as you think you are; your circumstances are as you believe them to be, and what you think about, you bring about.

Like Attracts Like

Thinking positively attracts positive outcomes. Now, this is not to say that sitting around daydreaming about all the great things you want to come your way in life will make them materialise as if by magic. Thinking positively leads to taking positive actions, and it's through those positive actions that you achieve what you want. The key thing to realise here is that it takes positive thoughts to drive positive actions and, as you already know, your thoughts and feelings influence your perception of yourself and your circumstances. This means that outwardly saying you want to achieve something holds no power if inwardly you don't believe you can. *Saying* that you want to pass your driving test is of no value if inwardly you're thinking that you'll probably fail; *saying* that you want to quit your job and start your own business is of no value if inwardly you don't believe you have what it takes to actually do it; and *saying* that you want to save up the cash you need to fund a dream trip but inwardly doubting your ability ever to do it can only lead to your thoughts becoming a self-fulfilling prophecy. Like attracts like, but it's not just what you say that matters, it's what you believe and what you do that attracts positive outcomes. In this sense, you might think of it as being a bit like a battery – when you think positively, your thoughts charge up the energy in the universe, and when you think negatively, those thoughts deplete it.

On the topic of energy drains, have you ever found yourself in the company of people who seem to suck all the positivity out of any conversation or situation? They have a way of being down on everything, and no matter how good your mood is before you hook up with them, their negativity rubs off and you find yourself getting dragged down. There's a saying, 'misery loves company;' it means that miserable people like to share their woes with others to ensure that everyone around them is able to feel their pain. Being able to empathise with others is a good thing, but too much time spent in the company of misery will lead to their negative energy depleting your positivity.

But the world is not limited to energy drainers – there are energy boosters, too. Think of the people you've met that seem to generate a positive 'buzz' in a room and have a way of adding positivity to any conversation or situation. These people are putting positive energy into the atmosphere, and it positively charges the energy of everyone around them. Clearly, time spent with positive people is a good thing, making it important to step back and consider how the people you spend most time with might be influencing your thoughts, feelings, beliefs, and therefore actions. This is not to say that you should go through life turning your back on people experiencing tough times; it simply means making sure misery is not your only companion. You can be there for people who need to share their problems, but you also need to spend time with positive people who can give your mental energy a boost.

Be a Success Magnet

Think of a time when you experimented with a magnet as a child. Holding it over a mix of objects showed you what would and would not be attracted to it. People are human magnets; we attract the people and things in life that have an affinity with our thoughts and beliefs. Like attracts like and what you think about you bring about, so think of yourself as a success in the making and all that you need to achieve your goal will be attracted to you – you will become a magnet to success. What you focus on, you give energy to, so keep your thoughts focused on what you want, not what you don't want, and on what you *can* do, not what you can't. When you think positively, the positive energy you put out into the universe is returned to you, taking you closer to the outcome you want and bringing the things you need closer to you. Negative thinking, or saying you believe in something when, really, you don't, can only ever repel rather than attract the outcome you want.

Until your thoughts are focused on the life you see yourself living as the person you want to be, your thoughts can't attract those positive things into your life. Allowing your thoughts to dwell on everything you're unhappy about or about which you have doubts effectively turns your mind into a magnet trying to pick up a wooden stick. To attract the best outcomes, you need to be your best and give your best in all you think and all you do. Making your best efforts gives you the best opportunity to get the best return. You can see this yourself – just think about projects you embarked on half-heartedly. If you're not fully committed to making something happen, it won't, and if you're setting out with doubts over whether you'll see something through, you won't. Like attracts like, so you need to think about the things you want and *expect* good things to come your way. Successful people think successful thoughts. Successful people keep their focus on the positives of every situation, never allowing fear or doubt to sabotage their actions. Negativity demagnetises you; negativity drives the things you want away from you.

Each one of us is the person we are today because of the thoughts and actions of our past. Everything we believe, think, and expect shapes our lives. When you stop to consider this, you begin to realise that you can attract everything you want into your life by simply taking control of the thoughts you allow to run through your mind. Consider it some more and you'll realise that you can't be any more in life than you plan to be or do any more than you plan to do.

See Yourself as a Success

Success means different things to different people, so *your* success can only be defined by *you*. In knowing what it is you want to achieve; you're already taking a step towards achieving it and the *want* to do something adds power to your potential to succeed. However, getting what you want is always going to be inextricably linked to how strongly you believe you can have it. In effect, you can only get what you believe is yours for the taking.

For those with religious beliefs, it's perhaps easier to accept that whatever it is you need is already yours. There's a quote by Harriet Emilie Cady, 19th century homeopathic physician and author of *'Lessons in Truth'*, that sums this up beautifully: *"A desire in the heart for anything is God's sure promise sent beforehand to indicate that it is yours already in the limitless realm of supply.* " With this belief, the desire you feel to pursue a particular course in life might be considered your calling – that deep inner feeling that guides you in the direction of your true purpose. Of course, discovering your purpose can take time, and a bit of trial and error may be needed, but achieving your true potential and becoming the best you can be in whatever you choose to do in life comes down to believing that everything you need to succeed is available to you.

Whether you have religious or spiritual beliefs or not, believing in yourself and seeing yourself as the person you want to be, living the life you want to live, is key to making it your reality. Seeing yourself as a success is made possible through a technique known as visualisation. Used by top-level athletes for many years, visualisation (also known as mental imagery) is now used in all areas of life, and by anyone interested in realising their true potential. What it does is turn your dream life into a movie, with you in the starring role. The film begins with you as you are and in your current circumstances. It ends with you living your dream life as the person you want to be. In between, you act out in the movie the steps you took to turn your dream into reality. You create a clear image of what you want and then you show the actions you take to keep moving towards your goal, even when obstacles stand in your way.

The great thing about visualisation is that you can watch the film in your mind's-eye whenever you like, and you can skip backwards and forwards to whatever scenes you want to focus on. Life doesn't always go to plan, but if you don't have a clear plan you risk drifting. When you visualise your success you send out into the universe positive mental energy which will be returned to you in the form of the things you need. And being able to visualise how you will overcome the obstacles that are bound to get in your way helps to develop a powerful habit of positive thinking, giving your self-belief a boost whenever needed. Visualisation gives you what you need to awaken and inspire your inner lion and there's something very important there that often gets missed when visualisation is discussed. Many – perhaps most – writers about visualisation talk as though all that was needed was to visualise the final outcome. See yourself as you want to be when it's all over and, lo and behold, you will become that person. That ignores the truly vital middle step. You don't get what you want simply by visualising yourself with it – you first have to visualise all the steps on the way, and the problems and obstacles

Finding Passion and Purpose

But what if you're not sure of your purpose in life? What if you haven't experienced a calling; what if you're drifting through life feeling there's something missing that you just can't put your finger on, or what if you've reached a point in life where you feel stuck in a rut?

There's an inspirational way of thinking that can be traced all the way back to the ancient Norse people. They believed everyone has their own 'fire' within them and those who can keep that fire alive and carry it with them through life will achieve most in life. The fire represents a burning passion. As they saw it, the individuals destined to get most out of life were those who found something they loved to do and went on doing it. Using this as inspiration, you can discover your own 'fire' by taking a moment to ask: What do you love to do, and what fills you with enthusiasm? What gets you all fired up just thinking about it? What do you feel passionate about being or doing in life? What do you wish you could devote more time to doing – or wish you could do all the time? Answering these questions will help you find your passion and your purpose.

Of course, if you're feeling stuck in a rut, you might not feel fired up or inspired by anything and, without realising it, you might be drifting through life waiting for inspiration to come your way. Your inner fire has all but gone out, making it hard to visualise what it is you want out of life. At times like this, an 'inspiration board' can be a positive way to actively seek out the things that are going to relight your fire! Collect images or words that catch your attention. The images might be places, people, memorable moments in time, possessions, things you admire, or anything at all that sparks your interest. They can act as reminders of things you've loved to do or things that matter in your life. Is there a connection between them? Are they things you've enjoyed in the past, or are they forgotten dreams that were never realised? Remember, it's your life to live and your path to find, not the path someone else believes is the right one for you. If you feel there's something missing in your life, could it be that you've allowed the things you once loved to do and felt passionate about to fall by the wayside to concentrate on things you felt you *should* do, rather than *wanted* to do?

An inspiration board can help you to rediscover and rekindle your inner fire. All the clues you need to help you find what inspires you will be there, but sometimes it takes a physical visit to a meaningful location or time spent in the company of inspirational people to relight the fire. From there, visualisation allows you to *see* yourself being who you want to be and doing what you want to do – fulfilling your true purpose, and realising your true potential. When you find your inspiration, you also find the source of positive energy that makes you a magnet for success.

Imagine a whole new intake of first year university students arriving on campus. They're all going to explore what's available to them and they'll all gravitate towards their interests. Readers will be drawn to the library, and they'll find affinity with other book lovers, perhaps joining a book club; sporty people will be drawn to the gyms and playing fields and they'll find affinity with others who share their passion; arty people will be drawn into art circles; musicians will find other musicians, and those with little interest in study and much more interest in parties will soon find others with the same attitude. The way each individual thinks is effectively a mental magnet that attracts the things being thought about and others who think the same way. A magnet can only attract things like itself, it can't attract opposites, so the energy being sent out in a person's thoughts will attract the same energy in return.

The energy in your thoughts is yours to control. A mental magnet charged with positivity, love, kindness, gratitude, and sincerity will attract more of the same, but it can quickly become demagnetised by negativity, hatred, envy, jealousy, or anger, and will only attract more of the same. In short, the way you think attracts more of the same into your life. Love, kindness, and friendliness will attract love, kindness, and friendliness from others in return, but hate, anger, and suspicion will only ever attract hate, anger, and suspicion. The energy you put out in your thoughts is the energy you will receive in return, so getting more out of life begins with putting more in. Your life is a reflection of your thoughts, so charge your thoughts with positivity.

Passion and positivity are behind all success in life. The only limits in life are the limits you place on yourself, so the only obstacles holding you back are those created in your thoughts. If you spend your day thinking about everything you *don't* have, you are keeping yourself trapped in that place. If you dwell on things that haven't gone to plan, you're holding yourself back from moving on, and if you doubt yourself or consider yourself to be stuck with your lot in life, then stuck you will be. Until you think differently, nothing can change. Until you charge your thoughts with positive energy, positive things can't be attracted into your life. Visualising yourself living the life you want creates a positive energy that will attract the people and things you need to succeed. Only by seeing yourself being and doing better, and believing in yourself as that person, can you move towards that goal. Seeing and believing in what it's possible for you to achieve provides the spark that drives greater effort, and greater effort leads to greater achievement. In life, you can only achieve what you believe you can achieve, so when you build your self-belief a world of opportunities opens to you.

Passion Projects

In 2021, when the world was virtually at a standstill due to the Covid-19 pandemic, a survey conducted by the Open University revealed that female students were three times more likely than their male counterparts to be pursuing a passion project or a side hustle alongside their studies. Known as 'passion-preneurs', these students are inspired by hobbies and interests they love, and women in particular appear to demonstrate a 'go getter' attitude that allows them to juggle their student lives with their career ambitions. The study concluded that this generation of students is ahead of the game, displaying determination to get the most from both studies and passions; with sharp ideas about their future and where they want their career to take them, they're taking the steps now to make it happen. Another finding from the study is that today's university students expect to have three or more different jobs in their lifetime. This highlights a change in thinking from the days of a 'job for life' and indicates that young people are open to lifelong learning and exploring new ideas and opportunities that come their way.

Melinda French Gates is a good example of where passion and ambition can take you in life. She is known today as co-founder of the Bill and Melinda Gates Foundation, and she's ranked by Forbes as one of the most powerful women in the world, but she didn't set out in life from a privileged background. It was her ambition that drove her in her education and career, and that same ambition now drives her as a business leader and philanthropist.

Growing up, Melinda's father worked as an aerospace engineer in Dallas, Texas and her mother was a stay-at-home mum who came to regret not going to college. For this reason, her parents encouraged her and her three siblings to focus on their studies, saying, *"No matter what college you get into, we will pay for it."* Melissa's father created a side-line source of income in rental properties, and everyone in the family, including Melissa, helped to run and maintain the business by doing whatever jobs were required every weekend. When Melinda was 14, her father bought an early Apple computer to help with the family rental business and she took to it straight away, learning BASIC and then teaching her friends the programming language during school holidays. At Ursuline, the all-girls Catholic high school she attended, the motto is Serviam, translating from Latin as 'I will serve', and every student there is expected to get involved in volunteer projects, but Melinda was something of an all-round star pupil. Her former maths and computer science teacher has said of her, *"Every day she had a goal; the goals were run a mile, learn a new word, that sort of thing, but her ambition was never abrasive. Never. She was always lovely and charming, and she would win people over by being persuasive."*

During her freshman year Melinda discovered that only the top two students from Ursuline had earned places in elite schools. She says, *"I realised that the only way to get into a good college was to be valedictorian or salutatorian. So that was my goal."* She achieved her valedictorian goal, and her valedictory speech perhaps gave an indication of the philanthropist she would become: *"If you are successful, it is because somewhere, sometime, someone gave you a life or an idea that started you in the right direction. Remember also that you are indebted to life until you help some less fortunate person, just as you were helped."* She achieved her ambition of earning a place at an elite school, but a visit to Notre Dame University with her father led to disappointment as officials informed them the university was shrinking its computer science department, saying, "computers are a fad" – this was 1982! She chose to attend Duke University instead where she earned her BA, going on to achieve an MBA and then joining Microsoft in 1987. She was the youngest and the only female recruit in a batch of ten MBAs, but her ambition saw her rise to the position of general manager of information products within nine years before making the decision to leave the company and concentrate on family life – having married the company CEO.

However, Melinda's 'goal a day' ambition didn't stop there. Shortly after their wedding, the Bill and Melinda Gates Foundation was born. She describes herself as an impatient optimist and says the Foundation's primary goal is to improve equity in the United States and around the world, and eradicate the illnesses that cause the unnecessary deaths of hundreds of thousands of children in the developing world every year. Some two decades later, Melinda wrote in the Foundation's annual letter: *"Polio will soon be history. In our lifetimes, malaria will end. No one will die from AIDS. Few people will get TB. Children everywhere will be well nourished. And the death of a child in the developing world will be just as rare as the death of a child in the rich world."* This statement may seem hugely ambitious, but as Melinda says, *"What great changes have not been ambitious?"* It's perhaps not a goal that can be achieved in a day, but what Melinda says that really chimes with this book is that a goal is only a wish unless you have a plan.

Melinda French Gates has always been and remains a go-getter, and what we can learn from her story is that passion and ambition lie at the heart of her on-going success. Successful people don't always start out with a clear picture of what they will become successful at, but they all start out with a vision of becoming the best they can be, and they all believe in their ability to achieve whatever they put their mind to. The things you put your mind to are the things that inspire and motivate you, so they're things you feel passionate about and love to do. There are lots of successful individuals out there who have come to understand with the benefit of hindsight that the success they have in doing what they now do has come through always doing what they love to do. They may have tried various career paths and changed direction several times, but each choice will always be connected by something they love to do – something that has allowed them to keep their inner fire alive and carry it with them on their journey. The road to success is rarely straight and smooth. Twists, turns, bumps, and detours are part of life, but when you know in your heart where you want to go, everywhere the route takes you along the way is another step to getting there. The connections are there, and those connections will lead you from where you are to where you want to be.

To begin building a clearer picture of where you want to be, try asking yourself these questions and answering them with total honesty. When you get to where you want to be...

- Who will you be?
- Where will you work?
- What will you do?
- Where will you live?
- Who will you have around you in your life?
- What will you be most proud of?
- What will make you smile?

Honest and detailed answers to these questions will give you what you need to visualise yourself being that person and living that life. Use your inspiration board to give you visual reminders of things that matter and things you love to do, and this will help you to build an ever-clearer picture of where it is you're going. The positive mental energy generated through seeing and experiencing what you want becoming yours, will keep your inner fire burning bright, and keeping your focus on what you want will ensure that all the positive energy you put out into the universe will be returned to you and all you need to succeed will be attracted to you. To live the life you want, set yourself daily goals that matter to *you*, and keep Melinda Gates's voice of experience in mind: *"If I didn't fill my schedule with things I felt were important, other people would fill my schedule with things they felt were important."*

Chapter 3

Choose Happiness

"The grass is always greener on the other side." It's a common expression and it reflects the belief that all you need to be happy is to have a certain something. The 'something' could be a possession, a lifestyle, a certain amount of money, a house, a job, an opportunity... the list goes on. The problem with thinking like this is that you are focused on what you *don't* have in your life, and you see the unhappiness you feel as the result of not having that something. This kind of thinking gets no-one anywhere. There will always be an other side on which the grass seems greener. Whatever you achieve, that will always seem to be the case. But is it?

Say you're unhappy in your work. You believe that if you could just get the promotion you're after, you'd be happy. And then you get the promotion, and you may be happier for a while, but it isn't long before you're no happier than you were. So now what do you do? If you're like most people, you keep repeating the cycle of looking for the next something you need to be happy, and the happiness you think you'll find continues to elude you. Why? Because you're always looking for something more, rather than finding happiness in what you have.

Happiness Is a State of Mind

The key message here is that, if you're always looking for happiness in material things or 'certain somethings', you'll never find it – or you won't find *lasting* happiness – because there's always going to be something else. True happiness is found internally. It's in your thoughts and your frame of mind.

As long as you keep thinking about all the things you *don't* have, or dwell on all the things that *haven't* gone the way you wanted them to, your frame of mind remains negative, and negative thoughts can only ever lead to negative outcomes in life, keeping you trapped in a downward spiral of negativity because like attracts like. Of course, it's important to understand and accept that no one is happy all the time, not even those who always appear to be upbeat whenever you're around them. Everyone experiences upset and sadness at times in life, so setting out with the expectation of never feeling unhappy ever again is unrealistic. What you can aim for is to be able to put things into perspective. Negative things happen, but there are' positives to be found in every situation. All it takes to find them is a positive frame of mind or a change of perspective.

A good way of thinking about this is to consider the popular split between people who see the glass as half full and those who see it as half empty. Which type of thinker do you consider yourself to be? The natural tendency of glass half empty people is to adopt a pessimistic viewpoint and focus on negatives, becoming blind to positives in life. There's a saying, *"The optimist sees the doughnut, the pessimist sees the hole."* Some people say it was said by Oscar Wilde and that's possible – doughnuts certainly existed in his time – but there is no evidence that it was him and people often hang famous names onto quotations to give them a boost. Whoever said it, it expresses an important truth: What you focus on, you give energy to, so in the same way that thinking you're bored generates feelings of boredom, thinking you're unhappy generates feelings of unhappiness. In this state of mind, you're unable to see anything other than things that confirm your belief: you *think* you're unhappy, so you *feel* unhappy, and your perception of reality is that there's nothing to be happy about. Thinking you're happy, on the other hand, produces the opposite result. Isn't that strange – that just thinking you're in a particular mood can put you into it? But it isn't as simple as that, as we are about to see.

Everyone's definition of happiness is going to be slightly different and what makes someone else happy may not make you happy, but have you ever asked yourself if you're happy? That may be a question you ask others, or a question others ask you, rather than a question you ask yourself. It's quite possible that you recognise when you're *not* happy more readily than when you are happy, and there's a difference between feeling happiness in a particular environment or moment in time and feeling truly happy in yourself. As author Mandy Hale once said, *"Happiness is an inside job. Don't assign anyone else that much power over your life."*

We all want to be happy, and we want those we love to be happy, so how do we know if we are? It's true that happiness is a state of mind, but it's also true that, as humans, we're going to experience a range of emotions – not just happiness. Every emotion, including sadness, is part of life, and accepting that lows will come and go along with highs is an important step towards finding true, inner happiness. Sometimes you'll feel happy, sometimes you'll feel sad, and sometimes you'll feel every other kind of emotion in between, but *not* feeling these highs and lows would make you a robot.

Happiness comes to you when your expectations meet reality. Several wise people have defined happiness this way, and these words highlight how individual the meaning of 'happiness' is to each one of us. Being happy means being happy in ourselves; something that's not always easy to achieve. You might be someone who appears to have everything you could need to be happy – a loving family, a comfortable home, plenty of food and creature comforts, and enough money to buy fun things – but yet you don't *feel* happy. Having all the things you've been conditioned to believe should make you happy can lead to feelings of guilt creeping in when you finally admit to yourself that you're not. However, it's only by admitting how you're really feeling that you can begin to change how you're feeling. Pretending that you're happy when you're not can only ever keep you stuck in that 'not happy' place. Being true to yourself is an essential step on your journey to true happiness, and it's learning to love yourself just as you are. True happiness is found in liking yourself for who you are and what you believe in, not what others may have decided you should believe in, and in striving to be and do your best in all you do so that you can grow, flourish, and become the person you believe yourself to be as your best self.

Liking yourself is so much more important than having others like you, but in today's world of likes and followers on social media, it can be hard to deal with *not* being liked. It takes a lot of self-confidence for a young woman to walk to the beat of her own drum, but trying to be someone you're not in an attempt to fit in or be 'popular' is not being true to yourself – and lying to yourself as well as others can only ever hold you back from finding true happiness. When you like yourself as the person you really are, it becomes easier to see that someone not liking you is their problem and not yours. It's not about you, it's about them, and even though someone else's opinion of you can be hurtful, it doesn't need to influence or change the way you think or feel about yourself. Your happiness is yours – it's an inside job.

Of course, if you're not feeling happy in yourself, it's all too easy to begin comparing yourself to others, and especially those who seem to have the happiness in their lives that you want in yours. But hold on a second. Have you ever pretended to be happy when, really, deep down, you weren't? You'll be an unusual person if you haven't. How do you know that these people you're comparing yourself with aren't doing the same? Sending out images and messages that create an impression of 'living their best life' and being all they want to be? Trying to be more like them in an attempt to find the happiness they have will lead to disappointment, because they don't really have it. So what is real happiness? A good place to start is by saying what it isn't. True happiness isn't found in photo opportunities because it has to come from within. It's not found in all the gadgets, gizmos, trips, adventures, and so-called successes the media would have us believe to be the source of all happiness. It can only be found in being the real you. Connecting with others and sharing fun times with loved ones and friends can undoubtedly bring joy and happiness into your life, but true and lasting happiness is the happiness found in your connection to yourself as the real you, and in being and doing your best as you become your best self. The truer you are to yourself, the truer your connections with others become, and the greater joy they bring.

Young women face so many pressures from the outside world. These could be family pressures to live their lives a certain way; advertising pressures to look a certain way; social media pressures to be 'succeeding' in a certain way, and so on. The danger is that anyone who doesn't fit into the boxes they're being told they should want to fit into will doubt themselves or feel inadequate in some way. And that's a big danger because it applies to almost everyone. Society has changed, but even today women face an unspoken pressure to be married by a certain age, and anyone left 'on the shelf' is viewed with suspicion. There's also pressure to have a family, and this can create the added pressure of a clash between childcare and career ambitions. And how do you square to very conflicting ideas of success for women? One says that success comes from climbing the corporate ladder and securing top jobs. The other says it comes from being a mother and staying at home to raise a family. How do you know which path to follow, or which one will bring happiness? Certainly not by listening to other people. The answer to that question is inside you. Finding it begins and ends with knowing yourself and being true to yourself. Someone else's version of happiness is exactly that, someone else's. Your happiness is yours to discover for yourself.

Change Your Thinking, Change Your Life

Changing the way you see the world is a matter of changing how you perceive reality. (And if anyone ever tells you there's only one way to perceive reality, invite them to study the medical profession now knows about how our eyes and ears interpret the signals they receive.) We are back here to questions of optimism and pessimism and, if you're one of nature's pessimists, changing your perception of reality might seem like a tall order, but it isn't. The way you see yourself and your world is what is meant by your mindset, and your mindset *can* be changed. Psychologist Carol Dweck spent decades researching this topic and the effects of an individual's mindset on their potential to succeed in life. Through her work, the traits of having a fixed or a growth mindset were set out as follows:

Fixed Mindset:

In a fixed mindset, you believe that who you are is who you will always be. You believe that any abilities or skills you have (or don't have) are just the way things are, and there's nothing you can do to change any of it. In effect, you're stuck with your lot in life – for good or for bad.

Growth Mindset:

In a growth mindset, you believe that change is always possible. You believe that who you are now and the skills you have (or don't have) now are not fixed, and that everyone has the potential to achieve their own version of success with dedicated effort. You're *not* stuck with your lot in life.

The conclusion of Carol Dweck's research is that you need a growth mindset to have any hope of achieving your full potential in life. But if you don't have a growth mindset, you can develop one. A fixed mindset can only ever hold you back, but it's fair to say that most of us adopt a mixture of both mindsets at different times in life depending on the circumstances. The good news is that when you recognise yourself slipping into a fixed mindset, you can take steps to move into a much more productive growth mindset. How you view your circumstances at any given time is entirely down to your perception, and how you choose to deal with life's inevitable ups and downs comes down to your mindset. Your perception and your mindset are always your choice.

To put this into context, imagine you're job hunting, you apply for six positions, and you only get invited to interview for two of them. Does this constitute success or failure? If you're in a negative mindset, you're going to view the failure to get an interview for all six as a setback, but take a moment to consider how your invitation to two interviews will be viewed by someone who applied for six positions and wasn't interviewed for any of them. You see, a change of perspective can be all it takes to change your view of yourself and your life. Now imagine you go through both interviews, but you don't get a job offer. Now what do you do? If you have a negative mindset, you might slip into an attitude of 'things never work out for me' and wallow in self-pity. With a positive mindset, on the other hand, you remain open to seeing things differently. In a growth mindset, you accept that you didn't get the job, but you also accept that you did gain valuable interview experience that you can take forward with you and use to your advantage next time around. There are always positives to be found in every situation if you remain open to seeing them.

A very experienced sales manager once described a salesman's life to me. He said, "The best salesperson in the world – and who better than me to tell you this? – hears 'No' far more often than 'Yes.' Salespeople – even the best ones – get knocked back again and again. The good ones have a mindset that says, 'Every no gets me closer to the next yes.' They keep going, they get the orders, they meet their quota, everyone's happy. Including them.'

I said, "And what about the ones who don't do that? The ones who take 'No' as a personal blow?"

"They leave," said the sales manager. "They find something less demanding to do. Unfortunately, it's almost invariably also something less rewarding. But if you want life's big rewards to come your way – and there's no reward bigger than happiness – you need a positive mindset. You won't hack it without one."

Unfortunately, society once again has a way of leading us into comparing ourselves negatively against others, and this is perhaps especially true for young women facing all the pressures of having to look a certain way, behave a certain way, think a certain way, and generally conform to a set of preconceived ideas of what it means to be a woman – both in the workplace and at home. The world is always changing, and things have improved over the last few decades, but young women today can still find themselves up against old-fashioned and outdated points of view and opinions that can threaten to hold them back, or at the very least crush confidence. It takes self-belief to pursue a goal and commit to doing whatever it takes to achieve it when it feels like others around you are determined to stand in your way or undermine your every effort. This might rear its ugly head in the form of glass ceilings in the workplace or it might be in the subliminal messages of social media and the world of advertising but, either way, the outcome can be a gradual slip into self-doubt as you adopt the negative beliefs of others as your own.

Bigger Is Not Necessarily Better

Even when you're able to maintain self-confidence, the 'bigger is better' attitude that exists in almost all areas of life can generate an unhealthy atmosphere of extreme competitiveness. This also piles on the pressure to have more, do more, and just be more in general in order to experience the sense of happiness and satisfaction the world of advertising constantly promotes as the something we should all be chasing. When this becomes the backdrop to daily life, it's no wonder happiness continues to elude us because there's always something we don't have – and without it we can't be happy!

It's fair to say that, by today's standards, 'success' is measured mainly in terms of fame, fortune, and bling. On top of that, the success everyone aspires to is *instant*. Marketing campaigns promise 'instant happiness' or 'instant wealth' if we buy into their products, and the pressure to conform to certain ideals as a young woman continues to build with promises of 'instant weight loss' or 'instant love' if certain celebrity-endorsed programmes are subscribed to. All of this adds up to a brainwashing effect and the false belief that *not* having everything – and having it now – makes you a loser in life.

This is not to say that all competitiveness is a bad thing. In fact, life scientists believe that it's part of human nature to be competitive, something that began with our ancient hunter gatherer ancestors' need to compete for resources simply to ensure survival. If we weren't competitive, that argument goes (and it's almost certainly true), the human race would not have lasted as long as it has. Our innate ability to cooperate with others can also be considered a survival instinct because being part of a 'tribe' provided crucial protection. Of course, competing against others and competing against yourself are two very different things. Striving to have more simply to compete with others can't bring you happiness, but striving to be your best self can. True success can only ever be measured in terms of realising your *own* dreams, and finding your own sense of satisfaction in what matters most to you – no one else.

Changing Careers

Michelle Obama's story is a great example of finding your own sense of satisfaction in life, even when it means making changes of direction along the way. In interviews about her life and career, she has said, *"I was sitting in a sky-rise office, doing legal work that wasn't fulfilling to me, and I couldn't help but ask – what's it all for?... If there's some part of you that's questioning your career, it's important to listen to that. Our hearts sometimes know ourselves better than our minds do. For me, that meant pursuing a life of public service, a path I've been able to maintain since that major swerve. But even since I made that change, I've shifted roles and jobs as my life demanded it. There are times when you can work 60- or 70-hour weeks for less pay, and there are times when you may need to make more money or be home more consistently for your family. Knowing that at the outset – that any career change will probably be followed by more changes, in varying degrees – can help you keep things in perspective if and when you start to re-evaluate things once again."*

The former first lady is not the only successful woman to have listened to her heart and taken a 'swerve' in life. Ina Garten is a best-selling cookbook author, Food

Network TV host, and the former owner of the Barefoot Contessa speciality food store. In her 20s, she was working in the White House dealing with nuclear energy policy and management. From the outside, it looked like she had a great job, but Ina was left with the feeling that there had to be more to life, and something more fun than the career she was in. She says, *"Then I saw an ad for a specialty-food store for sale in the* New York Times, *and it was in a place I'd never been before: West Hampton. So my husband said, 'Let's go look at it.' To say that I knew nothing about what I was getting myself into was an understatement. I'd never run a business before, never even had employees working for me. But when I saw the store, I thought, 'This is what I want to do.' So I made the woman a low offer, thinking we'd have time to negotiate. But the next day she called me and said, 'I accept your offer.' That's when I said to myself, 'Oh, shoot. Now I have to run a specialty-food store.'"*

Another famous example of following your heart and doing what you feel passionate about is found in the story of Victoria Beckham's switch from pop star to fashion designer. Looking at her life from the outside, she appeared to 'have it all' and her life was the stuff of dreams for many young women aspiring to be singing stars. Of course, on the inside, Victoria felt unfulfilled, and clothes designing was her true heart's desire. In interviews about starting her business, she has said, *"I was very aware that people would have preconceptions because I was a Spice Girl, and I was married to a footballer. So I knew what people were thinking, but I really didn't focus on that. I was very focused on what I wanted to do I liked the fact that I didn't know a lot. Because knowing what I know now about the fashion industry, would I have had the guts to do what I did then? Probably not. I think I was quite innocent and naïve. There was a lot that I didn't know. I think that was good because I probably would have been terrified. The fashion industry is really scary, and I was a pop star, saying, 'Hey, I designed a dress.'"*

Jennifer Lopez has also become successful in more than one career. She is known as a dancer, an actress, a pop star, and a businesswoman, with interests in beauty, clothing, perfumes, and a production company, as well as her own charitable foundation. In an award acceptance speech, she once said, *"It has been an incredible journey of dreaming my wildest dreams and then kind of watching them come true. Music, acting, performing, this career has always been kind of an obsession for me... When people have said, 'You're doing too much, you can only do one thing,' I always had it in my mind, I was always a person who was like, 'why not?' So I kind of had to forge my own path and make my own rules."*

The Pursuit of Happiness

Okay, the main message here is that happiness isn't found externally, it's found internally. Nothing makes this point more clearly than the many stories of lottery winners who find themselves no happier with stacks of money to buy absolutely anything their heart desires than they were before their big win, and some even confess to being unhappier. This is backed up by research and the findings of several studies that have revealed true happiness is essentially found in 'doing good':

- Doing good deeds for others
- Doing things you're good at and that bring you joy
- Taking care of yourself and having a good work/life balance.

However, perhaps the most interesting finding to come out of these happiness studies is that happiness is a choice. Those who report the highest levels of happiness in life are those who choose to be happy with what they have at any point in life. This is not to say they're settling for what they have and choosing not to realise their true potential, it means they're choosing *not* to lose sight of all the good things they already have in their life – as happens when your focus is only on what you *don't* have.

There's a wonderful old folk tale that makes this point beautifully. It's known as *'The Wise Woman's Stone'* and the original author is unknown:

A wise woman who was travelling in the mountains found a precious stone in a stream. The next day she met another traveller who was hungry, and the wise woman opened her bag to share her food. The hungry traveller saw the precious stone and asked the woman to give it to him. She did so without hesitation. The traveller left, rejoicing in his good fortune. He knew the stone was worth enough to give him security for a lifetime. But a few days later he came back to return the stone to the wise woman.

"I've been thinking," he said, "I know how valuable the stone is, but I give it back in the hope that you can give me something even more precious. Give me what you have within you that enabled you to give me something more precious. Give me what you have within you that enabled you to give me the stone."

This brings us neatly to the well-known proverb: *The best things in life are free.* Another danger associated with an attitude of bigger is better is that envy creeps in all too easily. If you're being subliminally told that having a certain gadget, car, designer brand, etc., is the route to happiness, seeing others with those things when you don't have them might lead to feelings of jealously – an emotion that, unchecked, can destroy relationships with others. One way to check it is to remember that the best things in life are free. As the Beatles once sang, "Money can't buy me love…" and the love, support, and companionship of family and friends is priceless. Sadly, the pursuit of material possessions or fame and fortune have led many to abandon, neglect, or take for granted important relationships, and by the time they realise the error of their ways, it's too late. It is, however, important to note that 'free' doesn't mean free of any effort on your part. You can't buy the best things in life, but getting comes with giving. The more love you give, the more love will be returned to you, so the more happiness you bring to others, the happier you become in return.

Just as bigger is somehow mistakenly linked to being better, being busy is somehow linked to being more important. The busier you are in your life, the more important you must be, but the problem here is that 'being busy' doesn't always equate to doing anything that really matters. If you become so caught up in trying to be everything society says you should be in order to live a fulfilled life, you have no time to discover and enjoy the things that really bring you a true sense of fulfilment, and the things that really matter – your relationships with family and friends, health, mental wellbeing – may have gone before you realise it. Being busy or important *isn't* important, being happy and fulfilled is. This isn't to say that having a high-powered job or earning a large salary is a bad thing, far from it; it just means that, to find fulfilment, you need to set your own goals and then, crucially, remember to stop and enjoy the view at each stage on your journey towards achieving them. Think of it this way: there's absolutely no joy in having a prestigious job if you hate every minute you spend at work, and there's no happiness in having money to burn if you're lonely and have no one to share it with.

To bring positive things into your life, you need to think positively, feel positive about who you are and what you're doing, and then take positive action steps as a result, allowing you to continue growing and moving towards realising your true potential. Becoming the best you can be should never be at the expense of others. As research has shown, happiness comes from doing good deeds for others, not looking out for number one. If you're thinking selfish thoughts, harbouring jealousy, hatred, or other negative emotions, and behaving in a way that matches your negative outlook, the trouble you're expecting to find is all that will come your way. If, on the other hand, you choose to look for positives and to be happy with what you've achieved, you can see and be grateful for the many good things you already have in your life. Choose to go through your daily life taking note of all the things you have to be happy about, not things to be miserable about, and you'll very soon find happiness. Remember, happiness is a state of mind, and it's not something you should be putting on hold. Choose to be happy now, today, and choose to end each day with positive thoughts of three good things you saw or experienced that day, allowing you to wake up in a positive frame of mind for the new day ahead.

Once again, there's an old English fairy tale that helps to impart great wisdom on this topic. It's known as *'The Hedley Kow'* and it originates from Northumberland where the Hedley Kow was believed to be a tricksy creature with mischievous shapeshifting abilities. The version below is from *More English Fairy Tales*, compiled by Joseph Jacobs and published in 1894.

There was once an old woman, who earned a poor living by going errands and such like for the farmers' wives round about the village where she lived. It wasn't much she earned by it; but with a plate of meat at one house, and a cup of tea at another, she made shift to get on somehow, and always looked as cheerful as if she hadn't a want in the world.

Well, one summer evening as she was trotting away homewards she came upon a big black pot lying at the side of the road.

"Now *that*" said she, stopping to look at it, "would be just the very thing for me if I had anything to put into it! But who can have left it here?" and she looked round about, as if the person it belonged to must be not far off. But she could see no one.

"Maybe it'll have a hole in it," she said thoughtfully: –

"Ay, that'll be how they've left it lying, hinny. But then it'd do fine to put a flower in for the window; I'm thinking I'll just take it home, anyway." And she bent her stiff old back, and lifted the lid to look inside.

"Mercy me!" she cried, and jumped back to the other side of the road; "*if it isn't brim full o' gold* PIECES!!"

For a while she could do nothing but walk round and round her treasure, admiring the yellow gold and wondering at her good luck, and saying to herself about every two minutes, "Well, I *do* be feeling rich and grand!" But presently she began to think how she could best take it home with her; and she couldn't see any other way than by fastening one end of her shawl to it, and so dragging it after her along the road.

"It'll certainly be soon dark," she said to herself "and folk'll not see what I'm bringing home with me, and so I'll have all the night to myself to think what I'll do with it. I could buy a grand house and all, and live like the Queen herself, and not do a stroke of work all day, but just sit by the fire with a cup of tea; or maybe I'll give it to the priest to keep for me, and get a piece as I'm wanting; or maybe I'll just bury it in a hole at the garden-foot, and put a bit on the chimney, between the chiney teapot and the spoons – for ornament, like. Ah! I feel so grand, I don't know myself rightly!"

And by this time, being already rather tired with dragging such a heavy weight after her, she stopped to rest for a minute, turning to make sure that her treasure was safe.

But when she looked at it, it wasn't a pot of gold at all, but a great lump of shining silver!

She stared at it, and rubbed her eyes and stared at it again; but she couldn't make it look like anything but a great lump of silver. "I'd have sworn it was a pot of gold," she said at last, "but I reckon I must have been dreaming. Ay, now, that's a change for the better; it'll be far less trouble to look after, and none so easy stolen; yon gold pieces would have been a sight of bother to keep 'em safe – Ay, I'm well quit of them; and with my bonny lump I'm as rich as rich – !"

And she set off homewards again, cheerfully planning all the grand things she was going to do with her money. It wasn't very long, however, before she got tired again and stopped once more to rest for a minute or two.

Again she turned to look at her treasure, and as soon as she set eyes on it she cried out in astonishment. "Oh my!" said she; "now it's a lump o' iron! Well, that beats all; and it's just real convenient! I can sell it as *easy* as *easy*, and get a lot o' penny pieces for it. Ay, hinny, an' it's much handier than a lot o' yer gold and silver as'd have kept me from sleeping o' nights thinking the neighbours were robbing me – an' it's a real good thing to have by you in a house, ye niver can tell what ye mightn't use it for, an' it'll sell – ay, for a real lot. Rich? I'll be just *rolling!*"

And on she trotted again chuckling to herself on her good luck, till presently she glanced over her shoulder, "just to make sure it was there still," as she said to herself.

"Eh my!" she cried as soon as saw it; "if it hasn't gone and turned itself into a great stone this time! Now, how could it have known that I was just *terrible* wanting something to hold my door open with? Ay, if that isn't a good change! Hinny, it's a fine thing to have such good luck."

And, all in a hurry to see how the stone would look in its corner by her door, she trotted off down the hill, and stopped at the foot, beside her own little gate.

When she had unlatched it, she turned to unfasten her shawl from the stone, which this time seemed to lie unchanged and peaceably on the path beside her. There was still plenty of light, and she could see the stone quite plainly as she bent her stiff back over it, to untie the shawl end; when, all of a sudden, it seemed to give a jump and a squeal, and grew in a moment as big as a great horse; then it threw down four lanky legs, and shook out two long ears, flourished a tail, and went off kicking its feet into the air, and laughing like a naughty mocking boy.

The old woman stared after it, till it was fairly out of sight.

"WELL!" she said at last, "I *do* be the luckiest body hereabouts! Fancy me seeing the Hedley Kow all to myself, and making so free with it too! I can tell you, I *do* feel that GRAND – "

And she went into her cottage and sat down by the fire to think over her good luck.

The old woman in the fairy tale knows true happiness. Her happiness is inner happiness that comes from choosing to be happy with what she has, but the last word on this subject must go to the Buddha and his famous quote that serves as a wonderful reminder to us all to be thankful for what we have on any given day or in any moment in time:

> *"Let us rise up and be thankful, for if we didn't*
> *learn a lot today, at least we learned a little,*
> *and if we didn't learn a little, at least we didn't*
> *get sick, and if we got sick, at least we*
> *didn't die; so, let us all be thankful."*

Chapter 4

Turn the Tide

Every plan you make in life is not going to work out just the way you want it to. That's just the way life is. The question is, how do you respond when things don't go your way? You can't control every element of the world around you, but you *can* control the way you deal with setbacks and disappointments. You already know that nothing is possible unless you believe it's possible for you, so now it's time to question how prepared you are to keep striving for what you want, even when it feels like everything is against you.

Retired soccer champion Mia Hamm once said, *"No-one gets an iron-clad guarantee of success. Certainly, factors like opportunity, luck and timing are important, but the backbone of success is usually found in old-fashioned, basic concepts like hard work, determination, good planning, and perseverance."* As the face of the Women's United Soccer Association, the first professional women's soccer league in the United States, Mia was a trailblazer in her career, twice becoming FIFA Women's World Cup champion and twice winning Olympic gold medals. Her determination to succeed kept her striving not only to be the best player she could be, but also to change attitudes in what was a male-dominated sport. Mia's passion for her sport inspired an entire generation of young women and girls to get involved and, thanks to her hard work, determination, good planning and perseverance, young girls following in her footsteps had the opportunity to become professional soccer players, allowing them to turn their own sporting dreams into reality.

You don't need to be a football fan, or a fan of any professional sport, to appreciate the years of dedicated effort and training it takes to make it to the elite level. Before Mia Hamm was known to the world, many young boys dreamt of becoming professional footballers, but there was no such thing as a professional football career for young girls to aspire to. She changed attitudes, not just in a sport steeped in tradition, but also in the minds of spectators. What her success shows is that change is always possible. She may have grown up being told that it was impossible for her to turn her passion into a profession, or that soccer as a career is 'not for girls', but she chose to play anyway, and through her self-belief she changed the long-held beliefs of others.

Failure Happens

Professional sport may revolve around winning or losing, but the important thing to remember is that losing and failing are different things. Negative things happen, but there are positives to be found in every situation. In sport, no one wins every competition, it's simply not physically possible to maintain peak fitness throughout an entire year, let alone an entire career, so progressive training plans are put in place to ensure appropriate periods of rest and recovery so that athletes can perform at their best when it matters most. Failing to win an event isn't failure when it's part of a training programme and a bigger plan. This is not restricted to sport; it applies in all aspects of life. What constitutes success or failure is never anything more than your perception of either state.

"Failure happens all the time. It happens every day in practice. What makes you better is how you react to it." – Mia Hamm

Everything in life is relevant to something else. If you're having a bad day, then it's only 'bad' because you're comparing it to a 'good' day; if you never experienced a bad day, then how would you know you were having a good day? When you think about it this way, without one there could never be the other. Without downs there could be no ups, and without failure there could be no success. This is not to say that to succeed you *must* fail, but simply that there can only be the potential to succeed if there's also the potential to fail. Note that accepting the possibility of failure is very different from *expecting* failure.

The Tide Will Always Turn

'This too shall pass' is an important message conveyed in several Bible passages. With or without religious beliefs, it's easy to see and accept that everything in life moves in natural cycles. The ebb and flow of the tide, the changing seasons, the phases of the moon are three from countless examples. Just as athletes train in progressive cycles of hard work followed by rest to maximise performance, farmers plant their crops in rotation to gain the best return from the soil, and it's this natural cycle of things that needs to be remembered when it feels like nothing is going your way. Armed with an acceptance and understanding of this natural way of things adds power to positive thinking through rough times because you know that better times will come around again. The highs and lows of life are just part of a natural and continuous cycle, and just as the tide will always turn and the seasons will change, so – when you maintain a positive outlook – can you emerge from setbacks and difficult times to once again enjoy good times .

Wallowing in self-pity maybe the tempting option when things are not going the way you want them to, but dwelling on the negative can only ever hold you back and delay the natural return to better times. What you think about, you give power to, so focusing your thoughts on disappointments and 'disasters' won't change anything or make things turn out differently. You can't change what has already happened, but you *can* change what happens next when you adopt a positive attitude. Anger, frustration, and despair are negative emotions that can keep you trapped where you are, prolonging your stay in a low. All it takes to begin your return to a high is a change of perspective. Look for the positives, learn from the experience, and take what you learn forward with you. We all know that what goes up must come down, but when you understand the natural cycle of things, you also know that when it comes to tough times, what goes down must also come up!

Be Your Own 'Boss'

You already know that positive thinking isn't a magic wand that can be waved to make everything go the way you want it to, but success comes firstly from believing it's possible for you to succeed and then from thinking and acting accordingly. Successful people believe in themselves, even when others don't. History is full of examples of creative people who carried on pursuing their dreams despite criticism, rejection, or initial failure. The belief they had in their ability to achieve what they wanted came from within, leaving no room for the doubts of others to become their own, and the positive thought process gave them all they needed to stay on track and not give up on their goals.

It's a sad fact that there are always going to be people around who seem to take pleasure in putting others down. They're ready and waiting with negative comments designed to undermine your every effort, and they'll tell you with great confidence that whatever it is you're aiming to do is impossible. It's hard not to begin questioning yourself when bombarded with this level of negativity. When others are doubting you, the negative energy they create can lead to the voice of self-doubt entering your mind and your thoughts, bringing with it a barrage of confidence-crushing 'what if?' questions: What if it all goes wrong? What if I can't do it? What if they're right and I'm making a fool of myself? What if I'm not ready? What if...? Self-doubt promotes fear, and fear can paralyze you. To get from where you are to where you want to be, you need to move, and it takes positive thoughts to drive positive actions. Banishing self-doubt is the only way to prevent fear from stopping you in your tracks. The key message here is that, while you may hear the nagging voice of self-doubt, keep two facts in mind: it doesn't have all the answers, and you don't have to listen. *Your* mind, *your* thoughts, *your* choices – be your own boss. With a positive attitude, negative 'what ifs' can be turned around. Instead of asking, "What if I fail?" you can ask yourself, "What if I succeed?" Focusing on what success will bring into your life sets in motion a positive cycle of thinking, feeling, and behaving successfully, and you choose to keep moving towards your dream.

Learning to control your thoughts is the secret of all happiness and success. The things you think about are the things you bring into your life, so thoughts of doom, gloom, and disaster can only attract more of the same. Turning your thoughts around to focus on what you want, not what you don't want, is the way to attract those good things into your life, but switching negative for positive isn't always so easy. A classic example of this is to ask yourself not to think of pink elephants. Did an image of a pink elephant flash into your mind as soon as you told yourself not to think of one? Research has shown that the harder you try *not* to think about something, the more likely it is that you will. In fact, it almost guarantees it! It seems paradoxical, but it's the way the mind works. Actively trying to avoid a thought leads to one part of your brain busying itself looking for other thoughts to focus on, but at the same time another part is keeping a check on this distraction or avoidance process to make sure it's being done properly. This draws attention to the very thought you're trying to avoid – and up pops the pink elephant you're *not* going to think about. To *not* think about something, your mind needs to keep remembering what it is you're not going to think about, and so the thought remains.

All of this highlights the importance of thinking in positive terms. Thinking in terms of, "When I'm successful I won't need to do this anymore", only draws attention to the something you don't want to be doing, so your thought process becomes negative. Thinking instead about what you *will* be doing when you're successful keeps your thought process positive. It is, though, unrealistic to expect to have total control over your thoughts at all times and never to allow a negative thought to enter your mind, and it's important to accept that a thought is just a thought. The key to taking control is to ensure that negative thoughts are just *passing* thoughts that you can push aside with thoughts of something much more productive. Dwelling on negative thoughts sends out negative energy that's going to be returned to you as more of the same, keeping you stuck there. Pushing them aside with positive alternatives ensures a return of positive energy that's far more useful. If you find yourself stuck in a place of worry, fear, anger, or any other negative emotion, step back for a moment and ask yourself if the thoughts creating the negativity are actually valid or necessary.

Thoughts that are obsessed over have a way of growing horns and getting blown way out of proportion, so one positive way of taking back control is to use a leaf out of Harry Potter's book. Fans of the magical stories will be familiar with creatures known as 'boggarts' that could turn themselves into an image of a person's worst fears. Harry and his fellow Hogwarts friends were encouraged to use the 'Riddikulus' spell to deal with them. This spell would take the fear out of the image by dressing it up in some ridiculous way. It may be the stuff of fantasy, but it demonstrates the very real power we all have to choose what we think about. We can choose to stay in a place of negative thinking, or we can choose to change those thoughts for positive alternatives. Thoughts *can* change, and changing a thought can be more effective than trying to avoid it completely. Psychologists liken trying to avoid thinking about something to trying to get to sleep or trying to concentrate. The more you try to force yourself to go to sleep, the less likely it is that you will because the process of trying keeps you wide awake, and the more you try to focus your concentration on one thing, the more likely it is that you'll find yourself distracted by every other small annoyance that you're trying not to be distracted by. Instead of trying not to think of a pink elephant, let the image appear and then let it go. The more you try to avoid it, the more you keep it at the forefront of your mind, so accept its presence and then choose to think of something else. A negative thought is just a thought, but what you do with it is always your choice.

Of course, just as there are people out there all too willing to crush the dreams of others, there are also people out there who seem to have no lack of self-confidence – yet they still 'fail' to get what they want. Good examples of this can be seen in TV talent shows such as *'The X Factor'* in which many positive thinking individuals confidently proclaim themselves to be the next big thing, only to find themselves rejected by the judges. In most cases, this leads to tears, tantrums, and wailing words of life being over. At the first hurdle in their path, these individuals fall. They may have *thought* of themselves as winners, but winners in life don't just think about becoming successful, they *act* on those thoughts and put action plans in place. Self-belief is not self-delusion, and thinking positively is not looking at life through rose-tinted glasses. Winners in life *commit* to doing whatever it takes for as long as it takes to succeed, and the journey to what you want is not guaranteed to be a straight or a smooth one. Obstacles in your path are only journey-ending roadblocks if you choose to view them as such; positive thinkers find a way around or over them.

Be a Trailblazer

Being a trailblazer doesn't have to mean blazing a whole new trail that makes the world sit up and take notice. It can simply mean having the courage to follow your own path in life. Breaking away from convention and traditional ways of thinking or doing things can be challenging, but only through setting and pursuing your own goals can you realise the life you want. Remember, successful people do what they love and love what they do, and many, like Mia Hamm, continue to do what they love despite so-called voices of reason discouraging them or telling them they're wasting their time. They choose to trust in themselves, and while they're always open to advice from knowledgeable and supportive others, they listen to the 'gut feeling' that lets them know they're doing what's right for them.

J.K. Rowling wanted a career as a novelist, but her parents tried to advise her against it, fearing that writing would never be a job that could pay the bills. She persevered, but failed to get through the entrance exams for Oxford University. Her parents no doubt hoped this would lead to a change of career choice, but she stuck with her dream and applied to other universities instead. Writing was her passion, but after leaving university she had to work in a string of temp jobs just to make ends meet. Her heart wasn't in any of her jobs and no offers of permanent employment came her way, so she carried on flitting from position to position, all the while keeping her idea for a novel alive and starting the writing process. Nothing in her life appeared to go to plan, and two years later, only three chapters of her book had been written. Now a single mother with no job, no money, and no book, she has often said in interviews, *"By every usual standard, I was the biggest failure I knew." She could have given up on her dream and accepted that her parents' fears had been justified, but in her heart she still believed that writing was the one thing she was good at. The end result was* Harry Potter and the Philosopher's Stone, *a book that was rejected 12 times before a publisher finally accepted it. The rest, as they say, is history. Something that's particularly interesting about J.K.'s story is that had she not found herself to be a 'failure' in so many other areas of life, she may never have had the time or the inclination to finish her novel. It may have become a dream that was put on the back burner and forgotten. She says, "Had I really succeeded at anything else, I might never have found the determination to succeed in the one arena I believed I truly belonged." What we can take away from this is that failure (and in this case, rejection) is never a reason to give up on what you believe in your heart of hearts you can achieve.* Finding a way through failure makes you mentally and emotionally stronger, giving you what you need to learn, move on, and do better next time. In J.K. Rowling's case, doing better meant becoming the world's highest paid author and the UK's best-selling living author.

When you know in your heart of hearts that what you're doing is what brings you a true sense of fulfilment, nothing can stand in your way – or at least nothing you can't find a way through or around. When you're pursuing your own goals in life, you put a best effort into everything you do, and there's no failure in doing your best. Not everything you set out to achieve is going to work out just the way you planned, but as the ancient Japanese proverb states, "Fall down seven times, stand up eight." There's no failure, there's only failure to learn and try again, and don't forget that the potential to succeed only exists because the potential to fail also exists.

Inspirational female trailblazers in history include:

Amelia Earhart – described as a 'rebel heart', Amelia was the first person to fly solo from Hawaii to the

United States, and the first woman to fly solo across the Atlantic Ocean. Her courage and passion for flying fuelled her adventurous spirit in a time when women were expected to aspire to little more than marriage and motherhood. She once said, *"Women, like men, should try to do the impossible. And when they fail, their failure should be a challenge to others."*

Babe Didrikson Zaharias – born in the early 1900s, Babe grew up with the goal of being 'the greatest athlete to ever live.' However, sexism and the societal norms of the times meant women were discouraged from competing in sports. In the 1932 Olympics, she won two gold medals and a silver, but far from winning her praise, she faced accusations of actually being a man instead, with one sports commentator going so far as to say, *"It would be much better if she and her ilk stayed at home, got themselves prettied up and waited for the phone to ring."* Babe rose above it all and continued to pursue her passion, excelling in track and field, softball, swimming, figure skating, billiards, golf, and even football. She once said, *"Winning has always meant much to me, but winning friends has meant the most."*

Elizabeth Blackwell – born in England in 1821, Elizabeth's family would later emigrate to the US. In 1847, she wanted to put her private study of medicine to good use by seeking admission to a medical school. Most schools rejected her on the grounds of being female, and when she was finally admitted to Geneva Medical College in New York she found herself ostracised and harassed by the male students and even prevented from taking part in classroom demonstrations. Determined not to give up on her passion, she emerged from college ranked first in her class and became the first woman in the US to graduate from medical school. She is today considered to be the first woman Doctor of Medicine in modern times. She once said, *"It's not easy to be a pioneer – but oh, is it fascinating!"*

Choosing to follow your own path or blaze a trail takes self-belief, but when you know what inspires you, what lights your fire and fills you with joy, you know you're on the right track. Choosing your own path is choosing to recognise your inner lion and set (and reset) your own limits in life. The only real limits you have are not those set by convention or society, they're the ones you set yourself, and the overriding message in this chapter is that, no matter what obstacles you face, maintain a positive attitude and the way forward will come to you. The last word on this topic must go to a beautifully succinct old Chinese proverb:

"Those who say it can't be done should stay out of the way of those doing it."

Chapter 5

Move Mountains

Self-belief is key to achieving your goals in life. No matter how big or small the goal, those who achieve are those who believe. Successful people have faith, and faith can move mountains. Faith is having total trust, whether in a higher being or in yourself, and an unshakeable belief that whatever it is you dream of doing *can* be done. With faith, you have courage in your convictions, and with faith comes hopefulness and positive expectation.

Basketball legend Michael Jordan once said, *"You must expect great things of yourself before you can do them."* These are wise words. No matter how big the 'great things' may be, or how impossible others may believe their achievement to be, with faith and positive attitude you have what you need to achieve the outcome you want – you can move mountains.

Faith In You

Another famous sports legend once said, *"Everyone needs something to believe in. It's lack of faith that makes people afraid of challenges, and I believed in myself."* These words were spoken by boxing champion Muhammad Ali, an iconic character known for his positivity and bold statements. He also used to make the point that he wasn't bragging because he always did what he said he was going to do! As you know, what you *say* you're going to do or what you *say* you believe in has no power unless your actions match your words. Positive thoughts drive positive actions, but negative thinking, or not truly believing in the things you say you believe in, can only ever hold you back.

In saying that faith can move mountains, you're saying that truly believing in something can make the seemingly impossible possible. What constitutes a 'mountain' is an individual thing, but it's a challenge or a task you're facing that feels huge. The thought of attempting to move a mountain is overwhelming, making it all too easy to give up without trying at all, but with faith you remain optimistic and hopeful, and you roll up your sleeves to begin doing whatever it takes for as long as it takes to achieve what you want. You believe you have what it takes, or that what you need can and will be yours if you stay positive and do your best in all you think and all you do.

Be a Bumble Bee

The story of Mary Kay Ash is one that demonstrates the power of self-belief and its ability to move mountains. Recognised today as one of America's greatest female entrepreneurs, she founded Mary Kay Cosmetics Inc. in 1963 – a time when women in the workplace were rarely promoted above secretarial roles. By the time of her death in 2001, the company had over three million independent sales agents across 35 countries and an estimated value of around $2.6 billion, so it's fair to say that she rolled up her sleeves and put her faith in her ability to achieve whatever she put her mind to. One of Mary's most famous quotes is: *"Aerodynamically, the bumble bee shouldn't be able to fly, but the bumble bee doesn't know it, so it goes on flying anyway."* In the male-dominated business world of the 1960s, she was the bumble bee that shouldn't be able to fly – but she went ahead and flew anyway.

As a child, Mary had grown up with the responsibility of caring for her father who had tuberculosis while her mother worked long hours to support the family. The responsibilities and difficulties she faced were often daunting, but her mother guided and encouraged her by saying, *"You can do it, Mary Kay. You can do it."* Her dream was to become a doctor, no doubt influenced by her experience of caring for her father, and her 'you can do it' upbringing saw her graduate from high school. However, her parents couldn't afford to send her to college, so at the age of just 17, Mary Kay married. When World War II broke out, her husband left to serve in the armed forces, leaving her at home with three children to support, a challenge she rose to with her 'can do' attitude by selling books door-to-door.

The war took its toll on the marriage, and soon after her husband's return in 1945, they were divorced. Mary Kay had been hugely successful as a door-to-door salesperson, so she now took a job with a direct sales firm to support herself and her young family. Her continuing success soon found her head-hunted by another company and her marketing skills quickly put her into the role of national training director. But, after 25 years of hard work in the direct sales business, her success had yet to be acknowledged by her supervisors and Mary Kay left the company when one of the men she'd trained was promoted above her and given double her salary.

This was the 1960s and Mary Kay believed that she was living in a man's world. After quitting her job, she planned to write a book to help women succeed in the workplace. Beginning by writing a list of everything she felt the companies she'd worked for got right and another highlighting areas where she felt there was room for improvement, it soon became clear that what she'd actually created was a business plan for her dream company.

In 1963, at the age of 45, Mary Kay put her $5,000 of savings into turning her plan into her business – a business designed to help women achieve unlimited opportunities for personal and financial success. With the help of her son, she opened her first Beauty by Mary Kay store in Dallas and her dream began. With dedication, determination and hard work, Mary Kay turned her small business with a sales force of nine into one of America's largest direct selling cosmetics companies with an independent sales force of millions. She did it with the 'you can do it' attitude passed on to her by her mother and she said, *"Sometimes I wonder if my mother was aware of the seeds she was planting in my life as a child and where they would take not only me, but thousands of other women. What she sent into my life I sent into others'. And they in turn have sent what they have into many lives as well."*

Mary Kay Ash's story is about having faith. Her faith in herself to be and do better moved mountains, not only for herself but for all the other women she inspired to have faith in themselves. She chose not to settle for the business world's view of a woman's role; she believed in herself, her ideas and abilities enough to blaze a whole new trail. In her words, *"In the heart of every successful person is, 'I can.'"*

See Your Strengths

Most of us slip into moments of self-doubt from time to time, and anyone claiming to have no fear of anything is probably kidding themselves. It can be hard to stay positive when facing challenges, and no one is immune to the occasional negative thought, but choosing to turn your focus to what you can do rather than what you can't is the most effective way to ensure that negative thoughts are only ever passing thoughts. This can be done in an instant by changing negative what if? questions into positive what if? questions. You know that by changing the energy of your thoughts, "What if I fail?" becomes, "What if I succeed?" and by thinking positively, "What if I succeed?" soon becomes, "I *can* succeed," and then, "I *will* succeed." The confidence to move from one state to the next comes from taking a look at the skills you already have and then having faith in your ability to use what you have to gain whatever additional skills you need to achieve what you want.

Doubt is rooted in a lack of self-belief. If you're in the habit of telling yourself that you won't be able to do the things you want to do, you won't be able to do them. If you've allowed yourself to take on the doubts of others concerning your abilities, then those doubts will undermine your efforts because those efforts will be half-hearted. Only consistent thoughts have power, so what you habitually focus your mind on becomes your reality – and it cuts both ways. What you think and say must be congruent with what you believe and what you do. Random thoughts have no power, so the message here is that telling yourself you can be whoever you want and do whatever you want in life is of no value unless you believe and have faith in these words: repeating positive affirmations in the mirror each morning is of no benefit unless you believe what you're saying.

Of course, getting from where you are to where you want to be is going to take time. Believing you *can* get there is essential, and then maintaining a positive attitude with each step you take helps to keep you moving towards your goal. This is where focusing on what you can do and what you already have rather than what you can't do and what you don't have holds most power as you develop a habit of positive thinking. Successful people have successful habits, and you can develop your own...

- Use the power of positive self-talk and positive affirmations. Make it a daily habit. The key to real success here is to really believe what you say.
- Make it a daily habit to be thankful for all the positive things you already have in your life.

Recognise the skills you already have and celebrate every achievement and success, no matter how small.

- Use visualisation to see yourself as the person you want to be, and have faith that you are this version of you in the making.
- Create a vision board of everything becoming the best you can be will mean in your life. Reflect on it daily to inspire and motivate your every thought and action.
- Surround yourself with positivity by reading books and listening to music with a positive message, and find inspirational quotes that resonate with you.
- Believe in yourself and your ability to achieve your dreams, and behave each day as the person you dream of becoming. Be your best and do your best and you will become your best.

Building Belief

Achievement begins in the mind. Until you believe in your ability to do something, it can't be done, and your achievements in life will never rise above the level of faith you have in yourself. To be more, you need faith in your ability to become more. Self-belief and self-confidence go hand in hand. To succeed, you need confidence in yourself and belief in your ability to achieve what you want. Building your belief can be thought of as anchoring a cornerstone building block in the foundations of your success. Other building blocks you need to succeed include knowledge, skill, experience, and attitude.

Knowledge:

Knowledge is power. Acknowledging what you already know and understanding that what you don't know can be learned is a powerful way to eliminate any doubt that comes from fear of the unknown. Increased knowledge brings increased confidence. But remember that you can't know what you don't know unless you remain open to trying and discovering new things, so the way to keep growing is to develop an on-going love of learning.

Skill:

Identifying what you're good at and where your strengths lie can be very empowering. Focusing on and developing your strengths can be just what you need to maintain your confidence when challenges come your way.

Experience:

The more you experience, the more knowledge you have. Every experience in life can be learned from, and while it's common to hear that we can all learn from our mistakes, it's important to note that just as much can be learned from our successes. Accomplishing any goal, big or small, builds confidence, and any 'failure' is merely a stepping stone to being and doing better.

Attitude:

Developing a positive attitude is essential for success. When you believe that change is always possible, you have what you need to remain optimistic through life's inescapable ups and downs. Combine attitude with experience and nothing will be able to prevent you becoming your best self and achieving whatever you put your mind to.

Female Firsts

Putting all the above building blocks together creates strong foundations to develop true self-confidence and self-belief. From this rock-steady platform, unshakeable faith can be yours – and faith can move mountains. Be a bumble bee. Don't stop to listen to those saying it's impossible for you to fly, just fly – and fly high. You can't expect anyone else to believe in you unless you believe in yourself. Just as Mary Kay Ash's belief in herself and her abilities allowed her to realise her dreams and inspire millions of other women to believe in themselves and what they could achieve, your belief in yourself is your own powerful source of inspiration.

When something hasn't been done before, it takes faith and courage to believe that it *can* be done, and that *you* are the one to do it. Throughout history, women have demonstrated the power of faith in themselves to achieve, and their achievements have inspired many more to believe in a world of possibilities.

Marie Curie – her scientific discoveries in the field of radioactivity have positively impacted cancer treatments. In 1903, she became the first woman to win a Nobel Prize and also the first female professor at the University of Paris. In 1911, she became the first person ever to win a second Nobel Prize.

Elena Lucrezia Cornaro Piscopia – in 1678, she became one of the first women to receive an academic degree from a university and the first to become a Doctor of Philosophy. Her achievement paved the way for women to not only receive an education, but to study and excel in subjects that interested and mattered to them.

Svetlana Savitskaya – as the first woman to go into space twice (1982 and 1984), she became the first woman to perform a spacewalk, spending over three hours cutting and welding metals outside the Salyut Seven space station.

Kathryn Bigelow – in 2010, she became the first woman to win an Academy Award as best director for her thriller war film *'The Hurt Locker'*. In the long history of the Oscars, only four female directors had ever been nominated for this award.

Margaret Thatcher – in 1979, she became Britain's first female Prime Minister, a position she held until 1990, making her the longest-serving British Prime Minister of the 20th century.

One Stone at a Time

Jacinda Ardern became the prime minister of New Zealand in 2017 at the age of 37, making her the country's youngest prime minister in 150 years. She grew up in a small town where she saw children going hungry and without shoes, and it was this experience of hardship and inequality that inspired her to enter the world of politics. In interviews, she has said, *"Everything I've ever thought about doing has been, in some sense, about helping people... I never, ever grew up as a young woman believing that my gender would stand in the way of doing anything I wanted,"* and she strongly believes that the next generation should grow up believing in themselves as who they are and who they want to be, rather than conforming to some preconceived expectation of who and what they're meant to be.

What's interesting about Jacinda's leadership style is that she has made it to the top without the need to be anything or anyone other than herself. Just like Mary Kay Ash before her, Jacinda was acutely aware of the male dominated environment she was entering in her career, but she chose to change attitudes rather than change herself. She puts it this way: *"One of the criticisms I've faced over the years is that I'm not aggressive enough or assertive enough, or maybe somehow, because I'm empathetic, it means I'm weak. I totally rebel against that. I refuse to believe that you cannot be both compassionate and strong."*

Realising a dream is not an overnight process. Jacinda Ardern lost many elections on her journey to success, but every loss was another step along the way in the learning process that took her to where she wanted to be. To achieve the life you want, be prepared to roll up your sleeves, and as author Catherine Pulsifer once said, *"When faced with a large project, remember you move a mountain one stone at a time."*

Chapter 6

The Power of Belief

A Scottish folk singer called Gerry Rafferty wrote a song that started with this verse:

> *Out on the street I was talkin' to a man*
> *He said "there's so much of this life of mine*
> *that I don't understand'*
> *You shouldn't worry I said that ain't no crime*
> *Cause if you get it wrong you'll get it right*
> *next time.*

If you get it wrong, you'll get it right next time. If only every one of us could keep those thoughts in mind every minute of every day. Because, if you get it wrong, you *will* get it right next time. But only if you believe you were. You already know that with faith comes hope and positive expectation. Never underestimate the power of that positive expectation. If you *believe* that good things will happen for you, they will; so much so that positive belief can bring outcomes in life so unlikely they seem miraculous.

American athlete Wilma Rudolph is a great example. In 1960, she became the first American female to win three

Olympic gold medals in track and field. That on its own put her into the history books, but what made her story even more remarkable is the fact that she was born with health difficulties that meant she needed to wear a brace on her leg. The 20th of 22 children, Wilma battled scarlet fever, double pneumonia and polio as a child. She said, *"My doctors told me I would never walk again. My mother told me I would. I believed my mother."* What Wilma *believed* she could do, she did; had she *not* believed she could do it, she wouldn't have, even though her physical abilities would have remained unchanged.

Wilma's attitude echoes Mary Kay Ash's belief that in the heart of every successful person is 'I can,' the faith that can move mountains. Her story backs up the message in Chapter Two that successful people believe in their ability to succeed, they believe in themselves, no matter how far from their goal they may seem, and the message in Chapter Three that how you choose to deal with life's inevitable ups and downs comes down to your mindset. Just like Mia Hamm, she accepted that, as an athlete, failure is something that happens all the time. She once said, *"Winning is great, sure, but if you are really going to do something in life, the secret is learning how to lose. Nobody goes undefeated all the time. If you can pick up after a crushing defeat, and go on to win again, you are going to be a champion someday."*

Becoming a champion in sport may mean winning medals, but becoming a champion in life is becoming the best version of you it's possible to be. To succeed in life, you need to accept that failure is possible, and then you need unshakeable self-belief in your ability to be who you want to be and do what you want to do – if you roll up your sleeves and persevere. It's also interesting to note that, while athletics brought great joy into Wilma's life, she achieved an even greater sense of fulfilment in life after her retirement from competitive sport when she formed the Wilma Rudolph Foundation to promote amateur athletics for all. Through her own success, she inspired the success of many more young athletes, young women in particular, highlighting once again that the true source of happiness in life is bringing happiness into the lives of others.

Believe It to Achieve It

What comes through loud and clear from every story of success is that what *you* believe is what matters. If you believe in yourself, the doubts of others can't hold you back, but the reverse is also true; if you doubt yourself, it won't matter how many times you're told by others that you can do something, you won't believe it. Until *you* believe it, you can't achieve it.

Belief in something gives you confidence, and thinking confidently about something sends out positive energy that will be returned to you. In all areas of life, belief is the raw power that fuels all achievement, but it's fair to say that the world of door-to-door sales is a great place to see the psychology of belief in action. Many university students take on sales roles to help finance their studies or accommodation costs, but not many stick with it for long once they're through the training. The reason for this is generally that – as we've already said – the best salesperson in the world hears 'No' more often (usually far more often) than 'Yes'. It's a life of constant rejection. As each day goes by without a sale, the belief that they'll ever make one soon dwindles. Giving up becomes the easier option. For those that stick with it, the belief that a sale can and will be made remains, so how do they get through the rejection that crushes the confidence of others?

The answer lies in visualisation, positive thinking, positive affirmations, and *expecting* great things of yourself. Those that succeeded in sales roles reported using visualisation at the start of each day to see themselves making a successful sale. They mentally rehearsed every detail of the transaction – approaching the prospect confidently with a smile; seeing them smile in return and show an interest in the opportunity they were being offered; seeing them sign the contract and hand over a deposit; and then seeing the warm handshake as the transaction was completed. The visualisation could then extend to an entire day of positive transactions, leading to seeing a clipboard full of signed contracts and a high-five from supervisors at the end of the day. With practice, the visualisation process took no longer than 10 minutes each morning, and those that used it said it left them feeling excited and positively charged for the day ahead.

Interestingly, those that struggled to deal with rejection and finally gave up reported that they'd often meet up with their peers in coffee shops to share stories of misery and disappointment throughout their day or week.

What this demonstrates is that the negative energy created in the environment during those conversations was all that could be returned to them. Those that succeeded, on the other hand, would make a positive effort to steer clear of negativity, choosing to spend time with upbeat personalities and successful role models. They'd also ensure they only used positive language when talking to themselves, banishing any negative voices of doubt or fear that crept into their minds.

This often took the form of looking at themselves in a mirror each morning and giving themselves a positive pep talk. Positive affirmations such as, "I feel ready; today is a good day, and I have everything I need to make a lot of sales today," send out a positive energy that bolsters belief and confidence. Approaching a prospect with a calm, confident demeanour and a genuine smile creates a positive energy that attracts positivity in return. Compare this to a dejected, defeated demeanour and a forced smile, and the difference in energy becomes clear. Those that struggled reported frequent negative conversations with themselves. The voice in their head would say, "This is never going to work; I'm not cut out for this," and complain about the weather, the lack of prospects, and anything else that could be used as an excuse for their lack of sales.

Success came to those who maintained their belief that success *would* come to them if they continued to be their best and do their best every day. As a successful salesperson herself, Mary Kay Ash was a firm believer in living by the golden rule of always treating others as you'd wish others to treat you. She made this the foundation of her company, and her sales team were encouraged to imagine that everyone they came into contact with was wearing an invisible sign that read: make me feel important. Believing in yourself is treating yourself with kindness and respect, and this helps to take the sting out of rejections. As the old sales cliché goes, every no is just another step towards a yes.

Like sales, success in life can only be yours if you believe it's yours for the taking. With this attitude, every 'no' that comes your way in the form of setbacks and disappointments can be used as a stepping-stone to keep moving towards a 'yes' next time. The batting stats of legendary baseball player Babe Ruth are often used to back up this point. In his illustrious career as a player, Babe held the record for the most home runs *and* the record for being struck out more than anyone else. If strikeouts are 'nos' and home runs are 'yesses', he only achieved those yesses because he was prepared to go through the nos! In his words: *"Never let the fear of striking out keep you from playing the game... What do I think about when I strike out? I think about hitting home runs."*

The Psychology of Belief

Successful people believe in themselves as successes. In sales, approaching a prospect expecting to be rejected is all but guaranteeing rejection. The same applies in life. Until you expect to succeed, you are effectively guaranteeing that you won't. An experiment carried out by Dr Robert Rosenthal in the late 1960s threw up some very interesting results on the psychology of belief.

A group of teachers were told by the school principal that they would be assigned a group of students showing the greatest signs of intellectual growth and development. The students were to remain unaware of their selection for the study, and the teachers were to use the same curriculum followed by the other students.

The point of the study was to test the 'expectancy effect' in the classroom, also known as the Pygmalion phenomenon. The expectancy effect proposes that, when someone expects a person to perform a certain way, it causes the person to live up (or down) to that expectation. At the end of the year, the students who had been expected to show the greatest improvement *did* show the greatest improvement, but it was then revealed that these students had in fact been selected at random, not because of any signs of greater intellect. Dr Rosenthal's research suggests that expectations strongly influence performance. When teachers expect students to do well, they do, and when expectations are not high, performances reflect this. This could be because the lack of expectation leads to a lack of encouragement to be and do more.

Between 1944 and 1965, the British government demonstrated the damage the psychology of belief can do. That wasn't their purpose – what they thought they were doing was providing an education system suitable for children of different ability levels (which, let's face it, means all children). They hadn't wanted to cause so much damage to so many lives – but they did. How? They divided the public education system into three levels. From age five to 11, children were in primary school. Then they moved into secondary education. Those who wanted to, and reached the required education standard, could go to university at eighteen; otherwise, they were free to leave school at 15 that's what they wanted to do, or to stay on till 16 at which point they would take GCE (General Certificate of Education) exams at O (Ordinary) level. Then – still at their own option, though the school would have something to say about it, they could decide to stay for another two years to take the A (Advanced) level GCE exams that would get them either a higher-level job or a place at university.

But the level of secondary education they received was decided by something called the eleven plus examination. It decided which secondary school they would go to, and secondary schools were themselves divided by level.

Take Newcastle upon Tyne as a typical example. The pupils who scored the highest marks in their 11+ examination in the city would go to a grammar school. The grammar schools were expected to produce highflyers – people who would go to university or, if that wasn't what they wanted, leave school at eighteen with A-levels to get a better job than anyone from any other school who would have left at sixteen at the latest because A-levels were only available at grammar schools. Those who failed to get into grammar school in Newcastle would, in descending order of their 11+ results, go to a commercial school, a technical school or, at the lowest level, a secondary modern school. Commercial schools were supposed to produce candidates with O-levels for the clerical jobs that, before the spread of computers, were available in large quantities. Students from technical schools would go into jobs like draughtsmen (but not architects, because architects needed a degree and would therefore have been to a grammar school). And if their eleven plus score was so low that they ended up at a secondary modern, they were expected to become binmen or to work as machine operators, welders or fitters in the factories and shipyards that Newcastle had in large numbers in 1944.

You may notice that we seem to be talking here only about boys. And that was the first problem with this system – it was no longer fit for purpose because it still worked on the assumption that girls when they became women would only work until they found a husband (and that was supposed to be there number one goal in life). The girls' equivalent of the grammar school was the high school and high schools did send a handful of girls to university but most of them became nurses and shorthand typists or took clerical jobs in banks. Careers that they would be expected to bring to an early end in order to keep house and raise their children.

The second problem with the system was that some people develop later than others and someone who at the age of 11 had been sent to a secondary modern school might very well by the age of 13 or so have become a potential university student – but with no way to get there. And the third problem, which is really why I'm telling you about this in this chapter, was that the grammar schools streamed their pupils. A typical annual intake would be 120 boys or 120 girls (the schools were segregated after the age of 11). These, remember, would be the 120 boys or girls who had been found to be the very brightest their city had produced. And the grammar school would divide them into four groups – the A stream, the B stream, the C stream, and the D stream. How do you suppose the pupils placed into those streams felt about it? I will tell you.

Those in the A stream were treated by their teachers as the cream of the crop. Those in the D stream were treated by their teachers as the least talented. The dunces, if you like. And that's what happened. A streamers worked hard, achieved good results, and in many cases went on to university. D streamers gave up – they assumed they were no better than their teachers thought they were, and they mostly left school after five years with no qualifications worth having. But how did that happen? These, remember, were 30 of the brightest kids of their year in the whole city. How did everything turn out so badly for them? Doctor Rosenthal has already told you. Remember? He said expectations strongly influence performance. He said, when teachers expect students to do well, they do, and when expectations are not high, performances reflect this.

Eventually, the grammar schools realised that they were not doing the best they could by all their students. They still needed to divide their 120 pupils each year into four streams, but now named those streams differently. You know what happened? Suddenly, no-one saw themselves as the cream of the crop or as the dunces. The best pupils went on getting excellent results – but those who would previously have given up, now that they had no-one looking down on them and making it clear that they weren't expected to achieve anything, started getting very good results themselves.

What does it all mean? Believe in yourself. Set your goals high and believe that you have what it takes to get there. And get there you will.

"Men often become what they believe themselves to be. If I believe I cannot do something, it makes me incapable of doing it. But when I believe I can, then I acquire the ability to do it even if I didn't have it in the beginning." – Gandhi

The area of medicine is another great place to see the powerful effect of belief in action. The placebo effect is a scientifically recognised phenomenon, and medical research has shown that what a person believes about the treatment they're being given can hugely influence the effects of that treatment. This ties in with having faith in something and the hope and positive anticipation it brings with it. If you believe a treatment will help you, it will, but if you don't believe it will help you, it won't. This is the same treatment, whether it's a placebo or an actual drug, so the only difference here is your attitude to it. What you believe is your perception of reality, and in the case of medical treatment, what you expect of it tends to be the outcome you experience. It takes positive expectations to realise positive outcomes.

Don't confuse this with the old and well-known expression, 'Hope springs eternal.' When people say that, they are usually referring to something that's perhaps a bit of a pipe dream. The 'hope' is not really positive thinking or expectation – it's wishful thinking and wishful thinking holds no real power. You can wish for something, but you're not fully committing to making it happen. Success comes to those determined to do whatever it takes to make it happen. Wishful thinking and positive thinking are two different things, just as true self-belief is not self-delusion. It's a chain reaction. What you believe influences your thoughts and your thoughts influence the way you feel. The way you feel influences the way you behave and the actions you take, and it's those actions that generate outcomes. Wishing can't bring you what you want unless you *believe* that what you wish for can *and will* be yours.

Faith, hope, and positive expectation are at the heart of all 'miraculous cures' and without them there can be no hope of success in any area of life. Winners in life accept that losing is a possibility and successful people accept that failure is a possibility, but winners never dwell on losses and those who succeed never dwell on failures. If you've ever watched a top-level tennis match, you know that. A player makes a mistake. The best players – the real champions – people like Serena Williams and Roger Federer put it out of their minds immediately. Most players dwell on it for a few shots, and that costs them the match. At the very highest level in sport, the difference between the champions and the close also rans is never technical ability. The players who come second have the same skill levels as the players who win. What the winners have that the silver medallists don't is a firm belief that this is their game, their set and their match. Choosing not to dwell on failure is like choosing not to dwell on illness but instead to focus on what's good in life. This is an important element in improving outcomes as the positive energy generated by positive thoughts attracts positivity and good things in return. Of course, a positive mental attitude is not a cure all for physical ill health, and thinking positively does *not* mean wearing rose-tinted glasses or denying the reality of a serious health concern, but there's much to be said for the ancient Greek belief that it takes a healthy mind to maintain a healthy body.

The Stockdale Paradox

The need to balance optimism with reality is at the core of what's now known as the Stockdale Paradox, a concept coined by author Jim Collins and named after Admiral Jim Stockdale, an American military officer who was held captive for almost eight years in a POW camp during the Vietnam War. Despite being tortured more than 20 times, being denied any POW rights, and having no way of knowing whether he would ever be released or even survive to see his wife again, he never lost faith or gave up hope. He said, *"I never doubted not only that I would get out, but also that I would prevail in the end and turn the experience into the defining event of my life, which, in retrospect, I would not trade."* His ability to hold firm to this belief under the circumstances is remarkable, but the paradox comes in his understanding of why he survived the experience when others in the camp didn't, describing those who died as the most optimistic. He said, *"The ones who didn't survive were the ones who said, 'We're going to be out by Christmas.' And Christmas would come, and*

Christmas would go. Then they'd say, 'We're going to be out by Easter.' And Easter would come, and Easter would go. And then Thanksgiving, and then it would be Christmas again. And they died of a broken heart."

The lesson we learn from Jim Stockdale's experience is that you have to confront the reality of a situation, no matter how harsh. Unthinking optimism is a recipe for disaster. And that can be applied to any area of life, not just life in a POW camp. Self-delusion, denial, sticking your head in the sand, call it whatever you like, but choosing *not* to face reality and to hope all the unwanted stuff just goes away only makes the inevitability of *having* to face it more and more unbearable. What Stockdale did instead was choose to adopt a positive mindset *and* accept the reality of the situation he was in. He knew the situation he and his fellow prisoners were in was not good, but rather than endure it with blind optimism, he set about *doing* whatever he could to raise the morale of everyone and to increase their chances of survival. He said, *"This is a very important lesson. You must never confuse faith that you will prevail in the end – which you can never afford to lose – with the discipline to confront the most brutal facts of your current reality, whatever they might be."*

Learned Helplessness

When faced with a difficult situation, we'd all like to think that we'd set about finding a way to resolve or at least improve it, rather than simply enduring it or letting things go from bad to worse. However, research first carried out in the 1960s concluded that there is such a thing as learned helplessness. The theory has evolved over the six decades since then but, in a nutshell, the research shows that when some people find themselves in a situation they feel they have no control over, the tendency is to give in to it and to accept their fate rather than try to do anything to change it.

This is something that has been noted in a hospital environment. When people are confined to a hospital bed and they're told to ring for assistance when they need anything, they can develop a mindset of, 'I can't do anything.' As time goes on, the danger is that this thought process then becomes debilitating as the patient gives in to not being able to do anything and remains in this mindset when it's time to begin doing things for themselves again. They get stuck in the *not* doing and accept this as the way things are for them, even when the reality is they could be taking steps to improve their recovery.

In effect, learned helplessness can lead to any thought of taking control of a situation being considered pointless. An attitude of 'there's no hope' takes over. Without hope, all is lost. Imagine if Wilma Rudolph had adopted the belief of the doctor who said she'd never walk again. Had she given in to this thinking and chosen to accept it as her fate, she would never have walked – her belief would have become her reality. Of course, we know that she chose to believe her mother who told her that she *would* walk again, and it was her faith in this being her reality that allowed her to *make* it her reality, inspiring her to believe in her ability to be and do more.

The findings of learned helplessness highlight the importance of paying attention to the language you use when you're talking to yourself. If you're constantly telling yourself that you can't do something, you're talking yourself into believing that there's no point in even trying. You *believe* you can't, therefore you can't, but is it really the way things are?

Going back to the placebo effect, if you believe there's no treatment that's going to be effective, there is no treatment that's going to change what you believe to be your reality. You might even refuse to try anything new that's suggested. On the other hand, if you believe that there must be a way to improve your situation, your positive frame of mind keeps you open to trying new things and the positive expectation creates an energy that allows you to *keep* trying and to remain hopeful.

Nothing is impossible unless you believe it is, and with faith there is always hope. Of course, as the Stockdale Paradox teaches us, pretending everything is okay when it clearly isn't is not the way to get through tough times. Not every situation has an easy way out when you look for it, but if you see anyone doing any of the following things, chances are you're looking at someone suffering from learned helplessness:

- Avoiding situations in which the outcome can't be guaranteed, which means making avoiding potential failure more important than tri- for possible success.
- Being overly self-critical when they do something not very well, and choosing to believe it confirms

they never had the potential to perform well in the first place.

- After failing to achieve something, avoiding any other similar type of task, believing they're destined to fail there too, instead of thinking, "If I got it wrong, I'll get it right next time."
- Believing that however hard they try, things just never seem to work out the way they want them to.

It's easy to believe you have no control over the happenings in your life and you're therefore 'helpless' to bring about any change. It's also easy to believe the opposite – that you can control what goes on in your life and you can make changes. It's a matter of belief. Of having a growth mindset to achieve your full potential in life. Of swapping learned helplessness for learned optimism.

I Think I can

There's a popular children's book called *'The Little Engine That Could'* that teaches young readers about the power of belief. If you remember the story, it's about a group of big engines refusing to pull a heavy train over a steep and difficult hill because they think it can't be done. When the little engine volunteers to pull the train, the bigger engines laugh at the idea – but, chanting, "I think I can, I think I can, I think I can," the little engine chuffs away and proceeds to pull the train up and over the hill.

The original story that inspired this book was published in 1906. *'Thinking One Can'* was written to promote the idea of positive thinking among young readers, and the message in both versions of the story is that, just like the little engine, you can achieve anything you put your mind to. All it takes is an understanding of the power of belief and how to apply it. If you believe there are no limits to what you can achieve in life, there *are* no limits. As a child, the way you see the world is the result of beliefs passed on to you by people around you. Some of those beliefs will be helpful. And some won't. As you grow towards adulthood, you need to work out which is which. You are not other people, you are you, and what others believe to be true may not be true when you choose to look at it from your own unique perspective.

Before 6 May 6 1954, no athlete had run a mile in less than four minutes. Because no-one had done it, there was an assumption it couldn't be done. Even some medical experts said no miler would ever break through the four-minute barrier. But then someone did. On 6 May, Roger Bannister – a medical student – ran the distance in 3:59:4. When he did that, he broke the world record. But he also broke through something else – a limiting belief held in the minds of countless athletes. Within a few weeks of this phenomenal achievement, Roger Bannister's record was broken by an Australian athlete running an even faster mile. Athletes now believed the sub-four-minute mile to be an achievable goal, not an impossibility, and many more faster times followed as a result.

Helen Keller is another impossibility made possible. Born in the US in 1880, Helen lost both her sight and hearing at the age of just 19 months after an illness.

In going on to become an internationally recognised author and educator, she achieved what most people must have believed to be impossible. She learned to feel objects and associate them with words that were spelled out on her palm by finger signals. She then learned to read sentences by feeling raised words on cardboard, and to make her own sentences by arranging words in a frame. Learning Braille came next, and she then learned to speak at a school for the deaf. By placing her fingers on the lips and throat of a speaker while the spoken words were simultaneously spelled out on her palm, she learned to lip-read, and by 1904 she had graduated from Radcliffe College.

These remarkable skills had never been achieved by any blind and deaf person before her, so she began to write about her experiences with a view to having them published in women's magazines. This was at the time when polite society never mentioned blindness because it was associated with STDs, but *The Ladies' Home Journal* published her articles, and other magazines soon showed interest. Helen went on to write a number of books about her life and began lecturing with the aid of an interpreter to raise awareness as well as funds for the American Foundation for the Blind. She travelled around the world several times on lecture tours, and her efforts to improve the treatment of deaf and blind people played a large part in liberating many from asylums.

"A happy life consists not in the absence, but in the mastery of hardships... If you can dream it, you can do it." – Helen Keller

Facing Difficulties

If you ignore a problem, it does not go away – it gets worse. You can't solve a problem until you face it. You have to believe that there is a solution, and you have to believe that you have what it takes to find it. Otherwise, the problem will remain. Wilma Rudolph didn't stick her head in the sand and pretend she didn't have to wear a brace on her leg, she faced the difficulty head on and chose to believe that she could change her circumstances. Admiral Jim Stockdale didn't sit back and wait for it all to be over by Christmas, he accepted the grim reality of his situation and then set about doing whatever he could to survive it. In Helen Keller's words: *"Character cannot be developed in ease and quiet. Only through experience of trial and suffering can the soul be strengthened, vision cleared, ambition inspired, and success achieved."*

Changing the way you see the world is a matter of changing your perception of reality, but pretending your reality is something other than it actually is *not* facing up to difficulties.

There's a great quote by Yvon Chouinard, the founder of the Patagonia outdoor clothing company, which sums up the need to combine a positive mindset with a healthy dose of reality if you want to benefit from the phenomenal power of self-belief:

"There's no difference between a pessimist who says, 'Oh, it's hopeless, so don't bother doing anything,' and an optimist who says, 'Don't bother doing anything, it's going to turn out fine anyway.' Either way, nothing happens."

Chapter 7

Being All You Can Be

A friend of mine has a daughter. She's an adult now, and very well established in her career as a doctor, but I have known her father since before she was born. From an early age, she knew she wanted to be a doctor – but then when she was 10 they moved from the big city to a little country town, and she started at a new school. At the end of her first day, she told her parents she was going to be a nurse.

Her father said, "What about being a doctor?"

"Oh," she said, "boys become doctors. Girls become nurses."

"Who told you that?" And she named one of the young boys at her new school.

Her father told me later, "I don't mean this to be critical of nurses. I have an enormous amount of admiration for nurses. But she'd always wanted to be a doctor and I wasn't going to have some young oik tell her what she could and could not aspire to. If she went on wanting to be a nurse, I'd give her every encouragement – but it had to be what she really wanted."

So he moved her to another school. One for girls only. One with a head who taught all the girls in her care that, if they were prepared to work for it, they could achieve anything they wanted. And it turned out that being a doctor really was her first choice. One that she achieved.

When you ask a six-year-old what they want to be when they grow up, they'll confidently tell you with great certainty exactly what they intend to become. The question is, will their youthful self-confidence allow them to achieve their ambition? Sadly, the self-confidence to believe that anything is possible often vanishes during our teenage years and into adulthood. A young girl might dream of being an actress or a dancer, but then as she grows older, she lets the doubts of others become her own. She's told she's not tall enough; not graceful enough; not pretty enough... the negativity goes on, and her dreams get pushed aside. She might then choose to follow a different path, settling for a career that fits in with the 'norms' of society and pays the bills, telling herself that her acting and dancing dreams were just childhood fantasies. However, her passion remains buried deep within her, and she'll often wonder what her life might have been like if she'd followed her heart and had the courage to pursue her dream.

Finding Grit

Ralph Waldo Emerson once said, *"Few men find themselves before they die."* By this, he meant that very few people discover who they truly are or all they can be in their lifetime. Not becoming all we are destined to be or not realising our true potential is all too common. The confidence we have as children can be knocked out of us in many ways, whether it's taking on the negative beliefs of others or losing faith in our abilities after setbacks and disappointments. The question here is: What allows some people to stick with their dreams and push through difficulties to become all they can be while others give up? What is it that drives those who succeed to keep believing that they can and will achieve their dream even when it means enduring tough times to get there? The answer may be found in what's known as grit.

The concept of grit was researched and popularised by psychologist Angela Lee Duckworth. She says, *"To be gritty is to keep putting one foot in front of the other. To be gritty is to hold fast to an interesting and purposeful goal. To be gritty is to invest, day after week after year, in challenging practice. To be gritty is to fall down seven times, and rise eight."* The words 'grit' and 'determination' often go together, and dictionary definitions of these words include synonyms such as courage, resolve, and strength of character. All of these terms sum up the difference between those who see their dream as their destiny and those who give in to doubt and give up.

Grit gives you resilience, and it's resilience that lets you bounce back from upsets when things don't go to plan. Grit gives you the perseverance needed to stick with a goal that feels a long way off in life, and the resolve to find a way around difficulties that threaten to block your path, so it's grit that gives those who succeed the drive they need to be and do their best in pursuit of what they believe to be their destiny. If you've ever given up on something, you might think it's because you lack grit. Be like Serena Williams when she makes an unforced error and put that thought out of your mind. The truth is we're all born with an element of grit within us; some tap into it and others never discover it's there. Finding it comes down to finding your passion. Successful people do what they love and love what they do, and it's fair to say that unless you're passionate about what you do, you're unlikely to have the grit needed to stick with it and overcome whatever challenges come your way (and come they will). It's only through being prepared to push yourself that you can grow; it's only through being prepared to fail that you can learn to improve and move on from failure, and that's why you need to be doing something you feel passionate or purposeful about. Otherwise you're unlikely to see setbacks as experiences you can learn from, and you'll most likely give up instead.

It's grittiness that gives you what you need to deal with disappointments and still keep striving towards your goal. Developing grit is developing a positive mental attitude and a growth mindset, and it's choosing to adopt an optimistic and hopeful outlook in life. A gritty person believes they *can* achieve what they want and has the self-belief and self-discipline to keep putting in a best effort, keep looking for positives in every outcome, keep learning from every experience, and keep taking those positives forwards to do better next time.

Success Is a Journey

You often hear people talking about their life is a journey and, yes, it is something of a cliché, but things become clichés because they have a nugget of truth at their heart. Success is a journey, not a destination. On that journey, you don't want to be like the child in the car who never stops asking, "Are we there yet?' You avoid that by enjoying what you're doing. Whatever path you're on, you need to be enjoying the journey, and those who succeed in life are those who are prepared to take the scenic route. When you're in it for the long haul, you're prepared to do whatever it takes for as long as it takes to achieve your goals. You're prepared to persevere, to put in the practice needed to become your best, *and* you're prepared to accept that things won't always go to plan. It's when things are *not* going your way and you're facing setbacks and disappointments that you need grit and determination to stay the course. But there's a difference between being gritty and becoming obsessed with achieving a goal. Successful people don't just doggedly pursue a goal, they give themselves permission to change course as they navigate through changing times in life.

Refusing to give in is generally promoted as a good thing, and it is a good thing, but not at the price of becoming so intent on achieving one thing that you fail to see the bigger picture. This has been the storyline of many a Hollywood film in which the dad is so focused on meeting an important deadline at work, getting a big promotion, or running his business that he neglects his family and loved ones. He'll miss the birthday party, the school play, the parents' evening... all the time thinking that everything he does is for his family, but his family have grown up and gone before he realises he hasn't been there for them. In film scenarios, it's usually the dad, but the same idea can be applied to anyone in real life.

Let's say you're like my friend's daughter, a young girl growing up with dreams of one day becoming a doctor. You've answered the question of what you want to be when you grow up with the same response for as long as you can remember, and you've heard your parents proudly telling other adults about your long-held ambitions. You've also been brought up not to be a 'quitter' and you've developed a degree of grit as you became a young woman, so you get your head down and work hard to achieve your goal, but as you begin to experience more of life, you begin to question whether a career in medicine is really what you want. In this scenario, the goal you've been doggedly pursuing may no longer be something you feel passionate about. Could it be that the ambition you thought was yours was actually an ambition your parents had for you? Could it be that you kept pursuing a long-held goal thinking that the sense of fulfilment you craved would come when you achieved it, only to find it didn't? A change of direction to follow your heart is *not* necessarily giving in. Grittiness can lead to tunnel vision or blind persistence, neither of which are likely to lead you to where your heart truly lies.

Sticking with a medical theme, the story of Florence Nightingale is perhaps a good example of grittiness and pursuing a dream that she believed was her calling. As a young woman of status in the 1800s, society's plans for Florence were nothing more than marrying well and becoming a mother. She, however, felt strongly that God intended her to devote her life to helping others, and her dream was to become a nurse. In Victorian times, women in upper-class circles were not given the opportunity to study at university or to pursue a professional career, but Florence was fortunate in that her father believed women should receive an education and he took on the role of educator himself. She studied Latin, Greek, Italian, history, and philosophy, along with mathematics and writing which were considered very unusual subjects for women to have any understanding of (or interest in) at the time.

In some of her published writings, it's clear that Florence felt strongly that the women she saw around her were conditioned into being virtually helpless, living lives that made absolutely no use of their education, and she was determined not to become caught up in that expectation. Having initially respected her family's wishes that she should aspire to nothing more than marriage, she eventually rejected the norms and chose to follow her own path. Gaining an education in the art and science of nursing meant hard work, but it also meant standing up against opposition from her family and society as a whole – it took grit.

Nursing and helping others was Florence Nightingale's passion. For her, it was her purpose and her calling, and knowing this gave her the grit she needed to stay the course despite resistance. Of course, not everyone has a strong sense of purpose from an early age, so where does grit come from when you're unsure of what it is you want to achieve in life? The answer is simple: Be curious. Keep trying new things, visiting different places, and learning along the way because the things you're most passionate about in life may be things you've yet to discover. Spend time with inspirational people and people with a determined attitude, and let their positive and hopeful outlook rub off on you. Don't let other people, or the dictates of society, decide the course of your life. Choose to follow your own heart, and if you begin to feel you lack grit, could it be that the goal you're pursuing is no longer a goal you're passionate about achieving?

Aim High

There's a wonderfully wise ancient Burmese saying: 'Who aims at excellence will be above mediocrity; who aims at mediocrity will be far short of it.' The message in these words is that unless you're pushing yourself to grow, you can't become any more than you currently are, and your true potential will never be realised, thereby echoing Michael Jordan's belief that you need to expect great things of yourself before you can achieve them.

In religious circles, there's a legend that helps to promote the idea that God intended man to live a life of growth, and that each one of us is born with the power within us to keep discovering ever greater possibilities and keep striving to become more than we are. It goes along the lines of, *"When God was equipping man for his long-life journey of exploration, the attendant good angel was about to add the gift of contentment and complete satisfaction. The Creator stayed his hand: "No," He said, "if you bestow that upon him you will rob him forever of all joy of self-discovery."* The message here is that there's joy in pushing the limits of what it's possible for you to achieve and that we should all experience the delight of pursuing goals we feel passionate about so that we can keep growing and keep discovering all we can be.

Champions in life recognise the champion within. Florence Nightingale felt a calling within her to be more than society expected (or, indeed, wanted) of her. Did she have everything she needed when she started? No. But she had faith in herself and her ability to acquire these things. Through her efforts to be all she could be, she paved the way for many more women to become more than they may have believed themselves to be, and the improvements made in the nursing profession improved the outcomes for countless more sick and injured hospital patients.

The drawback to all this is that hearing about people like Florence Nightingale can be intimidating. She had a calling, we think – why don't I? And the fact is that not everyone does feel a calling in that way, which this is why many people settle for an ordinary life, unaware of all the resources they have within them to live an extraordinary life. Many of the famous people we recognise as 'gamechangers' today didn't set out with ambitions to change the world. Sometimes it takes an incident, a chance encounter, an inspirational book, or an emergency or injustice to awaken the power and the passion. They always had it, but they didn't know they had it. It was waiting to be discovered. Back in the 1800s, author Orison Swett Marden wrote, *"The person who can write a book that will enable people to discover their unused assets will do an incalculable service to humanity."* Today, we have access to inspirational people and stories at our fingertips, and it's their achievements that often spark our own desire to pursue our dreams and question our true purpose.

Misty Copeland wanted to be a ballet dancer, nothing more. She not only achieved her dream; she changed the world of ballet. It wasn't her ambition to inspire change, she simply wanted to pursue her passion and to dance, making her an ordinary person who achieved an extraordinary life through her journey of self-discovery. A late starter at the age of 13, her abilities as a ballet dancer were instantly recognised, but historical and cultural norms were stacked against her. She didn't fit the profile in terms of background, body type, or race. Despite all of this, Misty became the first African American to be promoted to the highest role of principal ballerina, and through pursuing her passion and striving to be the best she could be, she changed the way the world imagines a ballerina.

Malala Yousafzai became the youngest person to receive the Nobel Peace Prize at the age of just 17. Born in Pakistan, she was brought up to value the importance of education by her father who was a teacher at a girls' school. In 2008, the Taliban seized control of her hometown and all girls were prohibited from attending school. Malala spoke up for girls wanting an education, leading to her being shot in the head. Her family moved to the UK where months of recovery in hospital followed, but Malala refused to hide away. She set up the Malala Fund, a charity dedicated to ensuring all girls have the opportunity to go to school, and earned the Nobel Peace Prize for her efforts. Malala didn't set out with thoughts of becoming an internationally recognised face of girls' rights, she just wanted to go to school.

In 1989, Tiananmen Square in Beijing, China became the focus of the rest of the world as TV footage showed tanks trundling through it after a violent crackdown on protestors. A lone man carrying shopping bags was seen standing in front of the line of tanks to block its path in an image that has become an internationally recognised symbol of resistance. Known simply as Tiananmen Tank Man, his identity and his fate remain unknown, but it's hard to imagine that he woke up that day knowing that he would face down the Chinese Army. As the events of the day unfolded, something within him rose up to give him the courage to do what he did, and stand up for what he believed in.

These stories of ordinary people achieving extraordinary things remind us that most of us will never know what we're capable of because we never put ourselves in a position to discover what we're made of – we choose the easy life over a life of pushing ourselves to be more. Heaven forbid that life should always be an uphill struggle; that's not what it's about. So what is it about? It's about staying curious and choosing to learn more, experience more, and try more. That's the only way to discover what you're really passionate about and what you're destined to become as your best self. It's fair to say that we're all conditioned to go through life in a fairly standard way – go to school; go to college or university; get a job; get married and have a family; retire, indulge our hobbies – and you may have subconsciously slipped into aspiring to nothing more because this is the path others around you have taken, a path that represents a comfortable life.

There's nothing wrong with comfortable, but what if there's *more*? You can't know what you're destined to achieve unless you push yourself to find out, and the more you find out, the more you find yourself. Finding yourself is knowing yourself as the real you, and recognising who you can become as the best you. Carved into the stone above the entrance to the Temple of Apollo at Delphi in Greece are two words that translate as, 'Know Thyself!' These words of wisdom are often attributed to the Ancient Greeks, but in fact they may belong to Ancient Egypt. What does it matter? Having appeared in different cultures and traditions at different times throughout history, these two words have always been revered as important, and perhaps as making the point that knowing yourself or finding yourself is the ultimate challenge and the peak of all knowledge. The poet T.S. Eliot wrote:

> *We shall not cease from exploration*
> *And the end of all our exploring*
> *Will be to arrive where we started*
> *And know the place for the first time*

Inspiring Greatness

Winners in life don't allow not having something to stand in the way of what they could have if they maintain a positive attitude. Hillary Clinton once said, *"There is a sense that things, if you keep positive and optimistic about what can be done, do work out."* Hillary Clinton was the First Lady of the United States from 1993 to 2001 but there have been many more firsts in this famous First Lady's life that have perhaps been overshadowed by events in her political career. Born in 1947, Hillary has been known to say that the unusual spelling of her name is down to her mother naming her after mountaineer Sir Edmund Hillary. Sir Edmund and Tenzing Norgay made history as the first men to scale Mount Everest, but that was six years after Hillary Clinton's birth, suggesting that this was not the case. In fact, it has since been suggested that her mother invented the story to inspire greatness in her young daughter. It would appear to have worked.

During her school days, Hillary was greatly inspired by NASA and the Space Race between the US and the Soviet Union. At around the age of 14, she wrote a letter to NASA to ask what she would need to do to become an astronaut, an indication that her mother's story had indeed inspired her to achieve great things, but the reply she received simply informed her that women were not accepted on the training programme. In high school, Hillary was class vice-president in her junior year but lost her battle for class presidency in her senior year against two boys, one of whom told her, "You are really stupid if you think a girl can be elected president." This was back in the 60s, but it seems that these happenings sparked her on-going drive to tackle gender inequality and her belief that staying positive and optimistic is the key to knocking down barriers and getting to wherever you want to go in life.

In today's world, it's hard to imagine that speaking up for women's rights was considered controversial when Hillary Clinton made her famous 'human rights are women's rights and women's rights are human rights' speech as First Lady of the United States at the United Nations Fourth World Conference on Women in 1995. However, it was another speech given in 1969 that began Hillary's string of firsts. As a student at Wellesley College, she became the first student ever to give a speech during commencement festivities; a speech that earned her a seven-minute standing ovation. She then graduated from Yale Law School in 1973, one of only 27 females in a class of 235, and became the only female on the President Nixon impeachment investigation team. In 1975, Hillary moved to Arkansas where she joined the Rose Law Firm. By 1978, she had co-founded Arkansas Advocates for Children and Families and been appointed chair of the Legal Service Corporation, the first female to hold the position, and then in 1979, she became the Rose Law Firm's first female partner.

Hillary's string of firsts didn't end there. In 1986, she was the first female to join Wal-Mart's board of directors, and in 1987, she became the first chair of the American Bar Association's Commission on Women in the Profession. In 2001, Hillary was sworn in as US Senator from New York, the first female to hold this position, also making her the first person ever elected to office after serving as First Lady.

In 2016, Hillary Clinton's dream of breaking through 'that highest, hardest glass ceiling' to become the first female US president may have been dashed, but her achievements continue to inspire women around the globe. Back in 1969 when she gave her speech at Wellesley College, she said, *"The question about possible and impossible was one that we brought with us to Wellesley four years ago. We arrived not yet knowing what was not possible. Consequently, we expected a lot... We arrived at Wellesley and we found, as all of us have found, that there was a gap between expectation and realities. But it wasn't a discouraging gap, and it didn't turn us into cynical, bitter old women at the age of 18."*

We all face challenges in life and all of us, at times, question what's possible, but something we can all learn from Hillary's achievements is that we can make change happen and make the seemingly impossible possible IF we remain positive and optimistic. In her words, *"You have just one life to live. It is yours. Own it, claim it, live it, do the best you can with it."*

Equal Opportunity

It's sometimes tempting to think the reason you haven't succeeded in the same way as someone else is that you haven't had the same opportunities. Everyone's circumstances are different, of course, and we don't all have the same talents, but we *do* all have the same opportunity to develop the talents we have. The difference between those who succeed and those who don't may lie in the way they use time. Time spent thinking about what others have and you don't, or what didn't work out the way you wanted it to is time wasted. Those who succeed choose to focus on what they have, and they spend their time honing their skills doing what they love and feel passionate about. Most importantly of all, successful people are true to themselves. They follow their heart, and they choose their own path, even when society would tell them that path is not for them. We each have equal opportunity to become what we are destined to be as our best selves.

Catherine the Great

The story of Catherine the Great is a powerful example of determination to fulfil a sense of destiny. Officially titled Catherine II, she ruled Russia for more than 30 years in a time that would become known as Russia's Golden Age. Her remarkable rise from humble beginnings in Germany to becoming the empress of Russia and the most powerful woman in the world is an extraordinary story of success that demonstrates her grit and willingness to play the long game to achieve her goal in life.

Catherine was born into the ruling Prussian family and baptised Sophia Augusta Fredericka. She was a princess, but there was very little money around. It was her mother's ambitions that saw Catherine presented as a potential wife to Peter III, heir to the Russian throne. She was 14, she didn't know a word of Russian, but she had a strong sense of her own destiny. In her memoirs, she wrote, *"The title of Queen rang sweetly in my ears."* She knew what she wanted, and she was determined to get it.

And so, when she was sixteen, she married Peter even though she found him boring and immature. He would eventually succeed to the throne as Emperor Peter III and she would be empress consort. She knew he would not make her happy, but she also knew Peter could never be an effective ruler and she would become the power behind the throne. From the moment she'd set foot in Russia, Catherine had worked hard at getting the Russian people to like her. She learned the language and converted to the Russian Orthodox Church. We know why she did that because it's in her memoirs: her mind was made up to do whatever it would take to one day wear the crown. Peter succeeded to the throne and was as disastrous a leader as Catherine had expected. She orchestrated a coup, forcing him to sign abdication papers. She became Catherine II after rallying the support of Saint Petersburg's troops and people, and began a reign that would span 34 years until her death.

Her ambition, determination and hard work gave her the prize she saw as her destiny, and she used her position of power to set about reforming Russia. She became an enlightened leader, not only expanding Russia's land and influence in the world, but also promoting art and education, helping to develop, enhance and strengthen Russian culture as we know it today. The first Russian university was founded, along with theatres, museums, and libraries, and though she ruled as a despot she was loved by the people as a benevolent leader. After her death, the country mourned publicly for six months.

We can't applaud everything she did, but her drive, ambition and leadership qualities are none-the-less admirable. She began preparing for her success when she was young, and she worked hard and courageously to achieve her ambition. Throughout her life and her reign, a great wind of change was blowing across Russia, but her strength of character and her vision of her own and her country's future allowed her to use her imagination to affect positive change, no matter how many headaches she endured along the way...

> *"A great wind is blowing and that gives you either imagination... or a headache.*
> – Catherine the Great

Sometimes we find ourselves looking for reasons *not* to push ourselves. Usually, if we take a good hard look at them, those reasons turn out to be excuses. What is really holding us back is fear of failure and the solution is: Everyone fails from time to time, so don't be afraid of it. Until you push yourself, you can't know what you're capable of. In chapter one, you learned that one of the most valuable things to come into anyone's life is that moment of learning that touches your soul and reveals the real you. That moment could actually be a moment of failure and, as long as it helps you discover an inner strength and resilience you didn't know you had, it simply doesn't matter. It's only through experiencing these challenging moments that you can begin to recognise and realise your true self and all that you can be. As Hillary Clinton once said, *"Never doubt that you are valuable and powerful and deserving of every chance in the world to pursue your dreams."*

Chapter 8

Attracting Prosperity

Like attracts like. You know that. Just focus for a moment on that word, 'attract'. Attract is what you're trying to do – you want to attract the right kind of friends, you want to attract success, you probably want to attract prosperity. (I say probably because that isn't everyone's goal. But as long as you have the other things you want, it's probably better to have them and be prosperous). All of those things – attracting the right kind of friends, attracting success, attracting prosperity – by now if you've been reading this book with any kind of attention you should know that they require one thing. They demand that you believe in your ability. Your ability to attract friends. Your ability to succeed. Your ability to be prosperous. You have to believe in them. Really believe. Your life ambition requires that you gain a particular qualification? Believe that you can. You'll still have to do the work, which goes without saying, but if you don't believe you can do it, all the work in the world may not get you across the line. Why? Because saying what you're going to do is not enough. You have to *think* you're going to do it. And you have to mean it. Without true belief, there's no commitment to making it happen, and without commitment, dreams will remain just that – dreams. Positive efforts attract positive returns, but if you're just paying lip service to something without backing it up with committed actions, your lack of real effort will prevent you from achieving any real results.

Whatever you dream of, define it. If it happens to be prosperity, for example, the first thing to be clear on is what prosperity means to you. It's fair to say that most people link prosperity with wealth and riches, but it has a broader sense which is more than monetary wealth; it's an overall sense of successfulness in all aspects of life. A prosperous person is flourishing, but flourishing doesn't have to mean stacks of cash in the bank. A prosperous person may be comfortable and financially secure, but their real wealth is in fulfilling their true potential and becoming the best they can be.

Think Rich

To be successful, you need to think successful thoughts, so to be rich, you need to think rich thoughts. Of course, your definition of success is unique to you, and the same applies to your definition of rich, but the key message here is one that has run through every chapter of this book: positive thoughts drive positive actions, and positive actions lead to positive outcomes.

There's a lot of dispute about who first said, 'If you don't like your life, you can change it.' I don't know who it was. But I do know that who it was doesn't matter; the only thing that matters is the thought. If the life you're currently living is not the life you want, you need to believe that change can happen. If you dream of success, but in your mind you're unable to believe that you'll ever be anything other than a failure, success will never come. If you dream of being fit and healthy, but in your mind you're already telling yourself that you'll never break out of your current unhealthy lifestyle, a slob you will remain. And, if you dream of financial security but inwardly you're thinking that you're destined to live a hand-to-mouth existence and that you don't have what it takes to better your circumstances, you can't prosper. Fear and doubt repel prosperity. What you think about, you bring about, so bringing about change begins when in your mind's eye you see yourself living the life you want, and you have a clear mental image of the person you will become. Only by changing your inward thoughts can you change your outward reality.

Mental imagery or visualisation was at one time most associated with elite sportspeople, but it's now used by anyone wanting to excel in whatever they do. In effect, it's using your imagination, so it's something any one of us can do, but getting the most out of it takes intentional practice. As a child, you probably created imaginary worlds in the blink of an eye and you may even have had imaginary friends, but for most of us using our imagination, or at least being spontaneous about it, gets harder as we get older. Take a moment to watch children play a sport. Football or anything else that is happening where you can see it. See how they find no difficulty in becoming their sporting hero. They run around, they pretend to be the hero, they *are* the hero. It simply happens for them. That's how visualisation uses imagination, allowing you to see yourself being the successful person you want to be. It gives you a sense of what's possible for you when everything you're aspiring to achieve comes together.

Do you know what you're doing when you visualise? You're communicating with your subconscious mind. You're creating images but you're also creating neural pathways. This is why sportspeople have had such success with mental imagery over the years as those pathways are connections between the brain and the muscles involved in the action being visualised. When you think about doing something and you picture yourself doing it, you create the same connections between your brain and the muscles involved as you would through actually doing it. The connection isn't as strong but it's still there. When you master the art of visualisation, you *feel* what you're focusing your thoughts on.

If you've ever felt nostalgic about an experience in life, it's the power of visualisation that's behind those feelings. Perhaps there's a place you remember visiting, and just thinking about it creates in your mind images of everything you saw. Those images then bring back the way you felt at the time, creating a picture that involves all your senses – the sights, sounds, smells, tastes, and *feelings* attached to the memory. Just thinking about an experience can generate a physical tingle of excitement, a wave of disappointment, a shudder of fear, or any other emotion felt at the time, because your imagination triggers the release of chemicals in the body that match how you remember the experience.

Being able to visualise something happening does not guarantee that it will happen. What it does is boost your potential to *make* it happen. Picturing yourself achieving your goal makes you feel good, and feeling good provides positive motivation to get on with doing whatever it takes to achieve it. The combination of thinking and feeling primes your brain, giving you a head start in terms of actually doing it in practice. In sport, a primed brain might mean faster reaction times, which might make the difference between winning or losing, but the same principle can be applied to whatever it is you aspire to excel at. Not having practiced something in your mind doesn't mean you won't achieve it, but practice makes perfect, and mental practice can only enhance physical practice.

Attract Prosperity

When you understand the power of visualisation, you realise why prosperity is repelled by fear and doubt. If you think of yourself as a poor person, unable to see your financial circumstances ever improving, you will remain poor. If you think of yourself as someone in poor health, unable to picture yourself ever enjoying good health, you will remain a poorly person. Until you can *see* yourself as the person you want to become and *believe* in your potential to make it happen, your negative thoughts will continue to bring only negative outcomes. Negative thinking can only ever result in repelling rather than attracting the outcome you want, and only by thinking of yourself as a success can you attract the things you need to achieve your goal. To attract the best outcomes, you need to be your best and give your best in all you think and all you do.

It's often fear of failure that holds people back, but in some cases it can even be a fear of success. Before stepping down in 2022, Sheryl Sandberg was the COO of Meta Platforms, a position she had held since 2008 when she became COO at Facebook. In her previous role, she was Vice President of Global Online Sales and Operations at Google, and prior to that, she was chief of staff at the US Treasury Department. In 2012, Sheryl became the first woman to be elected onto Facebook's board of directors, and she made it onto the *Times* 100 list of the most influential people in the world. By 2016, she was ranked number seven by Forbes in the World's 100 Most Powerful Women, but yet a question she often asked herself throughout all of this was, *"What would I do if I weren't afraid?"*

As such a successful and powerful woman, it's hard to imagine that Sheryl ever felt fearful of anything, but in her book *Lean In: Women, Work, and the Will to Lead*, she explains that a fear of success hung always over her. She believes this is true of many successful women. Her reasons reach all the way back to her school days. Having excelled in high school, her yearbook called her the student most likely to succeed but she had those words removed because she feared they would make her unpopular and she wouldn't get a date for the prom. She went on to win a scholarship in her first year of business school, but chose not to tell anyone about it, again through fear of this level of achievement making her unpopular. In her own words, she says, *"I instinctively knew that letting my academic performance become known was a bad idea... Being at the top of the class may have made life easier for my male peers, but it would have made my life harder."*

Sheryl's parents supported her academic achievement, but they also encouraged marriage. They believed it was important for a woman to marry young so that she'd get a 'good man' before they were all taken, and the fear of being left on the shelf meant Sheryl was married at the age of 24. She was divorced only a year later, leaving her with feelings of 'massive personal and public failure'. Fear had driven her decision to marry, and now divorce had left her so fearful of how she'd be perceived by others that, despite having a Harvard MBA and the offer of a job in Washington, she chose to move out to California to escape the shame.

Fast forward to 2008 and her new role at Facebook, where new boss Mark Zuckerberg told her that her efforts to be liked by everyone were holding her back. Sheryl realised he was right when he said that pleasing everyone wouldn't change anything, and she now says, *"Everyone needs to get more comfortable with female leaders, including female leaders themselves."* This realisation became the subject of a TED talk Sheryl gave in 2010, but even then, fear of exposing herself and fear of telling her personal stories almost prevented her from giving the talk in the way she did. She stood backstage and agonised over whether to open up or stick to the safety of statistics and academic studies. And then she asked herself, *"What would I do if I weren't afraid?"* She spoke honestly about the difficulties of being a career woman *and* a mother, and the heartache of having her young daughter cling to her leg and plead with her not to get onto the plane that day. The talk triggered an avalanche of positive feedback, spurring Sheryl to use her speech as the basis of her bestselling first book – a book that everyone around her said she shouldn't publish because it would be bad for her business career.

Sheryl could have listened to those negative voices, but she silenced them instead by asking herself what she'd do if she weren't afraid. She visualised herself actually being the person she wanted to be, giving the talk she wanted to give and achieving the outcome she wanted by being true to herself as her best self. She visualised *not* being afraid, and then she made it happen.

When you think positively, the positive energy you put out into the universe is returned to you, taking you closer to the outcome you want and bringing the things you need closer to you. If you're not fully committed to making something happen, it won't, and if you're setting out with doubts over whether you have what it takes, you're already setting yourself up to *not* have what it takes. Remember, like attracts like. To prosper, you need to believe in yourself as someone who *can* prosper.

Breaking Stereotypes

Although we are a lot closer now to equality in the workplace than we were even twenty years ago, many stereotypes still exist in terms of job and gender roles. Hillary Clinton was informed that women could not be astronauts when she wrote to NASA as a schoolgirl, and while that's no longer the case, there has yet to be a female president of the United States. Or, for that matter, a female leader of the Labour Party, though it isn't something the Conservatives seem to have a problem with. For as long as gender stereotypes continue to exist, women may find themselves being overlooked in certain careers, and it may even lead some young women to choose a different path because they fear sexism will limit their potential to achieve the role they want. To attract what you want, you need to believe without reservation that you can have it, and there are a growing number of women in the workplace breaking long-standing stereotypes and paving the way for other women to believe in their potential to excel in whatever field they choose.

Janet Yellen is one of them. In 2013, she became the first woman in US history to be Head of the Federal Reserve. Before her arrival in the role, banks were typically places filled with men in suits, and women were generally limited to admin or secretarial roles. She made history, but she also created limitless possibilities for women dreaming of high-flying careers in the banking sector.

Kristen Titus was the founding executive director of Girls Who Code and her mission is to encourage teenage girls into a still male-dominated tech world. She wants young women to see a place for themselves in the field of computer science, and is committed to closing the gender gap in one of the fastest growing job sectors.

The Pursuit of Happyness

Yes, I know that's not how you spell happiness, but *The Pursuit of Happyness* is the title of a 2006 film starring Will Smith as Chris Gardner. It tells the true story of Chris's year of struggling as a homeless single dad with a five-year-old son. Often forced to sleep rough in a train station, and facing a catalogue of daily challenges, Chris manages to hold down an unpaid position as one of 20 trainee stockbroker interns with hopes of earning the one full-time position on offer at the end of his internship. Despite his struggles, he never reveals anything of his difficult circumstances to any of his office colleagues, even lending one of his bosses five dollars to pay a cab fare when he desperately needed the money to care for his son. Sleeping rough, scraping together enough to fund a place for his son at a day-care centre, and studying for his stockbroker's licence exam, Chris's efforts are finally rewarded when he is awarded the full-time position.

This remarkable story demonstrates the almost miraculous power of maintaining hope. Despite what would have appeared to many to be almost hopeless circumstances with the odds stacked against him, Chris maintained his faith in himself to be and do better. He didn't dwell on his difficulties and never slipped into divulging any 'woe is me' tales to his colleagues. He chose to think and act as the person he believed himself to be, visualising himself in better circumstances, and by maintaining a positive outlook he attracted into his life the people and things he needed to become that person. Only a few years after his homelessness struggles, Chris founded his own multimillion-dollar brokerage firm.

Just imagine how differently things would have turned out if Chris had given in to thoughts of misery and despair... Thoughts of fear attract more fear; thoughts of worry attract more worry; anxious thoughts attract more anxiety; thoughts of hatred attract more hatred, jealous thoughts attract more jealousy, and thoughts of poverty attract more poverty. To succeed, all thoughts of failure need to be pushed aside by thoughts of success. What you think about, you bring about.

Pushing Through

Marissa Mayer is a former CEO of Yahoo, a post she stepped into after 13 years at Google where she had been one of the company's earliest employees and the first female engineer. Her appointment at Yahoo made her the youngest woman ever to lead a Fortune 500 company, and while her success in this post may be up for debate, there can be no denying that Marissa is someone who's not afraid to step up to a challenge. As she put it, *"I always did something I was a little not ready to do."*

Growing up, Marissa describes herself as painfully shy, yet she pushed through this to become captain of her high school debating team, the Spanish club and the pom-pom squad, as well as taking part in a wide range of extracurricular activities including ballet and piano lessons. Perhaps overcoming her natural shyness taught her how to do what she was 'a little not ready to do' but she says, *"I think that's how you grow. When there's that moment of 'Wow, I'm not really sure I can do this,' and you push through those moments, that's when you have a breakthrough. Sometimes that's a sign that something really good is about to happen. You're about to grow and learn a lot about yourself."*

Marissa graduated from Stanford University with degrees in symbolic systems and computer science. She had intended to major in paediatric neuroscience but switched to symbolic systems – a combined study of computer science, philosophy, linguistics, and psychology – which she describes as *"studying the brain without the gore."* After graduation, she had any number of job options open to her but chose to sign up with Google because she felt the company offered greater opportunities to be a part of the decision-making process. She explains her choice at the time by saying, *"I also interviewed at McKinsey, which is a great company, but I had some friends who went there, and they said, 'Well, we give the presentations, and then we leave the room, and the executives make the decisions'... I just felt like at Google I could be in the room. Even if you fail, you learn so much by being where the decision is made."*

When Marissa joined Yahoo, the company was struggling, and the first thing she wanted to do was change the culture. She wanted the people working there to feel valued, and she wanted to attract new recruits who would feel excited about joining the company, so she spent the first few weeks listening to people and building a picture of what could be done to generate a sense of pride in the workplace. One day when she was following her normal practice of being available to talk to people in the cafeteria, an employee asked her if it wasn't time to get to work. He said management took too long to make decisions. He was frustrated, and so were other people. He had some ideas, but no-one wanted to listen. This was exactly the attitude Marissa wanted. She set up a weekly forum where any employee could put forward an idea which would then be shared with the board. They'd get ideas, and the mystery surrounding management decisions would vanish. Something Google had taught her was that being 'in the room' and part of the decision-making process generated trust between employees and the board which, in turn, helped develop a sense of pride. Her leadership style and the decisions she made have since been criticised by many, but her answer to this is to say, *"One of the best pieces of advice I've ever gotten is there are always a lot of good choices, and then there's the one you pick, commit to, and make great."*

And that's how it is in life. You want to grow and prosper? There'll be choices to make and sometimes you will feel that you're not ready. Okay, so you're not ready. But forget that. Keep going. Push through those moments and you'll stay on track to becoming the best you can be. Visualisation is a valuable tool that helps you to see and experience the person you're becoming. As Chris Gardner once said, *"Only by acknowledging, 'Hey, here is where I am, and I'm here because I steered my horse here,' can I make the next choice to ride on out to the sunset where I'd really like to be."*

Chapter 9

A Healthy Mind in a Healthy Body

The Romans had a word for it. Well, five words, actually. And, since it was the Romans, the words were in Latin. 'Mens sana in corpore sano'. It means a healthy body and a healthy mind, and it didn't start in Rome – it goes all the way back to ancient Greek and Chinese civilisations. And it comes all the way forward to our time, too. Why? Because it makes complete sense. Five thousand years ago, they knew that a person's mental state influenced their physical state. We still know it today. Five thousand years ago, they knew that a person's physical state influenced their mental state. We still know it today. Good mental health and good physical health are inextricably linked together. Greek philosophers believed that it took a healthy mind in a healthy body to live well, and according to Thales, *"The happy man is the one who has a healthy body, a wealthy soul, and a well-educated nature."*

People who hate, people who envy, people who show contempt to others, people who seek only their own advantage at the expense of everyone else – those people can help us really understand the true meaning of prosperity, because they may acquire material wealth, but real health eludes them. What goes on in their minds infects their bodies. The soul Thales referred to means your inner self, so having a 'wealthy soul' means having an abundance of positive inner characteristics such as patience, kindness, generosity, and big-heartedness in general. With these traits comes sincerity and authenticity, and therefore an ability to be true to yourself and others. As for a well-educated nature, this suggests an on-going desire to learn and an open mind. If you want an active body, you also need an active mind. If you want an active mind, you also need an active body. What this all adds up to is that living well equates to being your best self – inside and out.

The connection between mind and body is worth exploring in a little more detail at this point because it helps explain why simply changing the way you think can lead to very real changes in your life. Changes you will like. It's not uncommon for people, especially when they're feeling low or hard done by, to slip into believing that they're fated in some way to never be anything more than they currently are or do any better in life than their current 'miserable' circumstances. In this frame of mind, a person might wish they could be anyone other than themselves, but they don't believe there's anything they can do about it because they see it as fate having dealt them a bad hand, or they believe themselves to be genetically disadvantaged in some way. The mind-body connection is widely accepted, but there's on-going research and debate over how and why this connection exists. For some, in the area of epigenetics in particular, the belief is that the character of our lives is determined by the cells in our bodies (all 50 trillion of them) and their response to environmental signals and changes, not genetics alone. What this means is that believing yourself to be genetically disadvantaged in some way, or that your genetic makeup is the 'reason' for your lack of health or success creates an environment in your body that matches your thoughts. In short, if you think you're unhealthy, unhealthy is what you will be.

The Secret Garden

Frances Hodgson Burnett published 'The Secret Garden' in 1911. It's considered a classic in children's literature. One of the characters in the book, Colin, is bedridden due to his belief that he has a 'hunchback' and will likely die young. Being hidden away from the outside world in his bedroom for years has left him self-centred and difficult to care for, and his servants are forced to give in to every demand due to his frequent hysterical outbursts. As the story unfolds, it becomes clear that the only reason Colin can't walk is that he thinks he can't. It's self-inflicted. When he eventually chooses to try standing up, he discovers that he can. His inability to walk was never physical, it was only his belief that was holding him back, and his legs are merely weak from years of lying in bed. He believed he was destined to die young, and he chose to wallow in self-pity. His servants believed he was too unwell to walk and treated him as an invalid, thereby adding to the general environment of ill-health surrounding him, and all it took to change his circumstances was a change of mind. The moment Colin believed he could live a healthy life; he began to get better. He had hope of a bright future, and his faith in his ability to improve his health allowed him to grow strong and flourish.

Sticking with classics, in the story of 'The Wizard of Oz', the lion believes that he lacks courage, the tin man that he lacks a heart, and the scarecrow that he lacks brains. They believe that finding the wizard will solve all their problems as the wizard will give them what they need. Of course, what Dorothy needs from the wizard is a way back home to Kansas, but as the story unfolds it becomes clear that each one of them already has within themselves the thing they believe they need the wizard to give them. On their journey along the yellow brick road, the lion often shows great courage, the tin man shows a compassionate heart, and the scarecrow who thinks he has no brain is an endless fount of good ideas but – because they don't believe they have these qualities – they don't recognise them when they happen. The original book, 'The Wonderful Wizard of Oz', was written by L. Frank Baum and first published in 1900. He says the story was written purely for family entertainment, but many life lessons can be learned from it, the overall message being that we should look within ourselves and not externally for what we need. At the end of the 1932 film adaptation, Dorothy says, "If I ever go looking for my heart's desire again, I won't look any further than my own backyard. Because if it isn't there, I never really lost it to begin with." Backyard in this sense can be interpreted as meaning 'self', reminding us that there's no need to seek validation, happiness, or love from anyone other than ourselves as we can find any and all of them by being the best we can be in all we think and do.

The lion, the tin man, and the scarecrow represent common doubts and fears many of us will experience throughout life. The characters' mistaken belief that they can't be who they want to be or live the life they want until the wizard gives them what they lack meant they only saw and experienced the world and themselves in the way they expected to see and experience it – lacking courage, lacking heart, and lacking brains. These characters, along with Colin, may be fictional, but they help to highlight the very real tendency many of us have to get stuck in a negative mindset, blinkered to anything other than events and happenings that back up our negative beliefs.

Healthy Body

When you're young, it's easy to take your health for granted. If you feel physically fit, then feeling mentally well automatically follows. When you *expect* to be full of energy and enthusiasm, you approach everything in life with an energetic and enthusiastic attitude. But what happens when things go astray? What happens when illness or injury prevent you from doing what you've always done?

The difficulties of dealing with setbacks is a subject that's very close to the heart of retired Olympic athlete Dame Kelly Holmes. In the 2004 Athens Olympics, Kelly won two gold medals on the track, and then chose to retire soon after at the height of her career. Since retiring, she has spoken openly about her mental health struggles, and in 2008 she founded the Dame Kelly Holmes Trust, "with a vision to get young lives on track using the unique skills of world class athletes to engage, enable and empower." As a schoolgirl, Kelly excelled at athletics, but academic subjects never appealed, and she left school aged just 16 to take a job in a sweet shop. After that, she worked as a nursing assistant before eventually joining the army. She started as a lorry driver, worked her way up to physical training instructor, and became a sergeant. While in the army, she won gold at the 1994 Commonwealth Games and silver in the European and World Championships two years running, but it wasn't until 1997 that funding gave her the opportunity to become a full-time athlete.

Now, at a time when she should have been in peak condition and able to realise her full potential, she was plagued with a string of illnesses and injuries. For the next seven years, full fitness eluded her and by the time injury struck once again just before the 2003 World Championships, she'd had enough. In her autobiography, she says, *"I thought: 'Why me? I'm so committed, so dedicated, why me?' I just looked in the mirror and hated myself. I wanted the floor to open up, I wanted to jump in that space, I wanted it to close, and I didn't want to go back out. I was in such a bad way. Then I started cutting myself... I was just so annoyed with my body, so annoyed with everything going wrong. I was hurting my body because it was really letting me down."* She kept all of this hidden, never telling anyone how she felt. The world of elite sport is about positive attitudes, focus, psyching out competitors by always being strong, and never bringing down the team around you. Despite the challenges she faced, her dream of winning gold at the Olympics stayed with her, and the following year she delighted a nation and amazed the world by winning two.

What's interesting about Kelly's story is the strength of mind she needed to battle through physical difficulties. Without the will to succeed, she would never have stayed the course to achieve her dream and realise her true potential, although in her own view she has yet to find her true purpose. A year after her double Olympic success, Kelly retired, but her mental struggles didn't end there. Without athletics, she felt lost, saying, *"When you retire, you go, 'Who actually am I?' because all you know is the athlete who wakes up in the morning, knows what's expected of them. Then you leave."* Finding her true self has led to openly discussing her mental health struggles and through her books, podcast, and work as a keynote speaker she hopes to inspire and empower others to push through their own challenges to find success.

At the time of Kelly's self-harm, being open about mental health issues was not encouraged and many people suffered in secret. Since then, the prevalence of poor mental health among elite sportspeople has been identified and steps have been taken to bring about positive change, but this is not just about sport. On-going studies have found that teenage girls and young women suffer worse mental health and wellbeing issues than their male counterparts, with twice as many girls as boys self-harming. Researchers from the University of Warwick have found that, 'gender inequality such as sexist notions around body type' are at the heart of the problem, along with other factors such as neglect, poverty, exam pressures, and social media bullying. A 2017 study published by the Association for

Psychological Science said that screen time and social media may have a bigger emotional impact on girls than boys with teenage girls and young women showing more concern over the way they look and how popular they are, often judging their own worth by how many followers and likes they have. The study concluded that there's a correlation between social media use and depression in girls that's not found in boys, and that further research is needed to identify connections between screen time, self-harm, and suicide rates.

Kelly's experience demonstrates the extreme highs and lows of her athletics career and the power of her mind to influence both states. Self-harm was an attempt to take control over a body she believed was letting her down, but dreams of Olympic success gave her the mental strength she needed to keep coming back from illness and injury, and keep putting in a best effort in pursuit of her goal. Without that goal, her life may have taken a very different path, and she's keenly aware of the negative impact retirement from sport can have on professional athletes. When sport is what you do, not doing it anymore can lead to questioning your purpose and worth. In effect, this is no different to a young woman looking in the mirror and questioning her worth in comparison to everything she's seeing on social media – if she's not being and doing everything everyone else appears to be and do, she must be failing.

Power Posing

Social psychologist Amy Cuddy became famous for her 2012 TED Talk on body language and how it can shape who you are. The results of her original study have since been shown to be flawed, but the idea of 'power posing' to boost self-confidence has remained popular. In her talk, she discusses the link between a person's posture and their self-confidence and performance in whatever task they're undertaking, and her belief that our perceptions of one another are influenced by body language and non-verbal behaviours. We judge people by the way they sit, stand, or hold themselves in general. This belief is certainly backed up in elite sport, for example by Kelly's determination never to show competitors any sign of weakness, but Amy wanted to test the 'fake it until you make it' theory using what is now known as power posing to see if standing strong could make you feel strong, and if acting powerfully leads to thinking powerfully.

Participants in the study were asked to hold either open, powerful poses, or closed, contracted poses for around two minutes. To picture a power pose, you need to picture 'Wonder Woman' in her classic stance: feet wide, hands on hips, head up, chin sightly jutted outwards. It's a strong, confident pose, and Amy found that after standing in it participants *felt* more powerful than those who hunched up, gazed at the floor, and tried to make themselves invisible. Feeling more powerful means feeling more confident, and confidence lets you trust in yourself and your abilities. The results of her research suggested that adopting a powerful stance could lead to signals being sent back to your brain about being open to trying things, whereas adopting a closed, powerless posture could send signals of feeling powerless, leading to powerless behaviour.

Amy describes power posing as faking it until you *become* it: *"Your body can change your mind and your mind can change your behaviour, and your behaviour can change your outcome."* It's fair to say that, when you lack confidence, adopting a power pose can feel fake, but further studies involving holding open, expansive yoga poses have shown that these 'power poses' can significantly decrease levels of stress hormones in the body while increasing levels of testosterone, a hormone linked to assertiveness and low anxiety.

Being Yourself to Become Your Best Self

'Faking it' isn't about trying to be someone you're not, it's about thinking and behaving as though you already are the person you want to become; the person you believe yourself to be as you become your best self. Amy Cuddy's research into power posing and the connection between mind and body was the result of her own experience with impostor syndrome. There had been many times in her life and career when she felt unsure of herself and her abilities, feeling that she didn't deserve to have the success she had and that she would be found out at any moment.

When first documented in the 1970s, impostor syndrome was most prevalent among high-achieving women, and while it's much better understood today, many successful women still find themselves doubting their worthiness. Whatever they have done, however hard they have worked, no matter how much success they have enjoyed, they feel like frauds. "I wasn't expected to do this. Therefore, I must be a fraud."

Research suggests that around 70 per cent of people will experience impostor syndrome at some point in their lives, and many famous women have talked about it in interviews. Lupita Nyong'o is an Academy Award winning actress, but she says, *"I go through acute impostor syndrome with every role. I think winning an Oscar may in fact have made it worse. Now I've achieved this, what am I going to do next? What do I strive for? Then I remember that I didn't get into acting for the accolades, I got into it for the joy of telling stories."*

Penélope Cruz, Helen Mirren, Sigourney Weaver, Kate Winslet, Jodie Foster, Emma Watson, and Natalie Portman have all spoken about feelings of doubt and inadequacy. These women are all seasoned actresses and household names, so it's hard to imagine that they should continue to doubt themselves and their abilities. And yet, they do. Emma Watson once said, *"It's almost like the better I do, the more my feeling of inadequacy actually increases, because I'm just going, 'Any moment, someone's going to find out I'm a total fraud, and that I don't deserve any of what I've achieved. I can't possibly live up to what everyone thinks I am and what everyone's expectations of me are.' It's weird – sometimes success can be incredibly validating, but sometimes it can be incredibly unnerving and throw your balance off a bit, because you're trying to reconcile how you feel about yourself with how the rest of the world perceives you."* These words echo the thoughts of many successful women, and highlight the importance of knowing yourself, being true to yourself, and following your own path in life.

In 2015, Natalie Portman gave a commencement speech at Harvard University where she had herself been a student. In it, she said, *"So I have to admit that today, even 12 years after graduation, I'm still insecure about my own worthiness. I have to remind myself today, 'You are here for a reason.' Today, I feel much like I did when I came to Harvard Yard as a freshman in 1999... I felt like there had been some mistake – that I wasn't smart enough to be in this company and that every time I opened my mouth I would have to prove I wasn't just a dumb actress. Sometimes your insecurities and your inexperience may lead you to embrace other people's expectations, standards, or values, but you can harness that inexperience to carve out your own path; one that is free of the burden of knowing how things are supposed to be, a path that is defined by its own particular set of reasons."* Again, her words highlight the difficulties many young women face in terms of feeling secure in who they are and confident enough in themselves and their abilities to forge their own path, not the path society suggests they should aspire to follow.

Helen Mirren uses self-doubt in a slightly different way. A more positive way. She has won more awards in her acting career than most, and she's known to global audiences for her performances on screen, stage, and TV. In 2003 she was given a Damehood for her services to drama, and she is on *The Times'* list of the top 10 British actresses of all time. She has earned her success, but self-doubt is still no stranger to her. She says: *"It would be wrong to think that you're always right and correct and perfect and brilliant. Self-doubt is the thing that drives you to try to improve yourself."*

Dealing with impostor syndrome may not be a one-time process, but the first thing you have to recognise it. Then, find ways to push through it. But take care. The effort can take its toll on your health and well-being. It can have a detrimental effect on your overall performance. It can lead to working harder in an effort to feel more worthy, and you may find you're setting yourself ever higher standards that become increasingly more difficult to maintain. Getting over impostor syndrome involves learning to accept that you have earned your success, and this becomes easier when your focus is on measuring your own achievements instead of comparing yourself to others. The girl who sat next to you in school is now a billionaire entrepreneur who in her spare time and for fun runs marathons where she regularly beats professional athletes? Well, that's great. Think yourself lucky to have such a splendid role model. Not for you – for other people. Because it isn't a competition. The fact that someone else is doing exceptionally well is not a reflection on you. You don't want (or you shouldn't want) to be a copy of someone else. You want to be the very best YOU that you possibly can. So don't look for perfection or being the best at every task. Change your mindset. Let yourself know that a personal best is good enough. Doing your best is all that's needed. It's not about how your performance compares to others; it's about how it compares to your performance as the best version of you – the performance you're able to see and experience through visualisation. Always doing your best allows you to become your best self.

Moments before her first race in the 2004 Olympics, Kelly Holmes was looking in a bathroom mirror, roaring at herself to, "Come on!" The roar was an empowering reminder to herself that she had earned her place on the start line, and she had put in the years of dedicated effort needed to put in a best performance on that day. Through positive self-talk, she mentally prepared herself to perform at her physical best. In the same way, Amy Cuddy used her power pose to remind herself that she had the skills and abilities to do whatever task she was facing, with the difference that, in physically preparing herself, she sent a positive message of preparedness to her brain. The mind-body connection goes both ways.

We all have the capacity to change our circumstances by changing our attitude to them. What you focus on, you give energy to, so an athlete focusing on an injury can only ever create in every cell in their body a negative environment that will slow down their recovery. By focusing on what *can* still be done rather than what they're being prevented from doing, they create a positive environment which speeds recovery and gets them back into training and pursuing their goals sooner. In all aspects of life, a healthy mind is a mind through which you maintain a positive outlook, and you are in control of your destiny. A healthy mind creates a positive, healthy environment in your body, and when you're feeling good, you're good to go wherever your heart desires.

Mind Over Matter

Faking it till you make it should never involve telling lies, but the story of American radio entrepreneur and self-made millionaire Cathy Hughes shines further light on the mind-body connection and how changing the way you think can change your life.

In the early stages of her radio station business, Cathy was struggling financially, and events appeared to be conspiring against her success. Her banker suggested she speak positively about her business and her situation instead of focusing on the negatives. Cathy says, *"He said, 'Lie. Say this is the best, I'm having more fun, I didn't know business could be so good, I may have to expand...'"* She thought it was a crazy idea and he must be joking, but he asked her to do him a favour and give it a try. The next day, someone asked her how business was, and instead of telling her tale of woe, she lied. She answered that same question from others over the next few days with the same lie, and before she knew it, people were approaching her in positive ways saying they'd heard her business was doing great. She says, *"I didn't notice I was making progress until I had turned the corner, and to this day the profits just continue to rise."*

Lying can't be condoned, and it's important to remember that 'faking it' *means* thinking and behaving as the person you want to become, or the person you believe yourself to be as you become your best self. However, it's possible to see beyond Cathy's lie to note that telling it undoubtedly changed her whole demeanour – and her bank manager knew this. The change to using positive language changed Cathy's energy, and positive energy was returned to her along with the people she needed to grow her business, making her lie a reality.

Setting Goals

Setting a goal is a tried and tested way to turn a dream into a reality. When you have a clear goal in mind, you can put in place an action plan to take you from where you are to where you want to be. The difficulty arises when the goal seems a long way off and motivation falters. To get over that, the goal needs to be a SMART goal – it needs to be Specific, Measurable, Achievable, Recorded, and Time-phased.

Goal setting can be applied to any aspect of life, but let's use professional sport as an example. It was always Kelly Holmes' goal to win Olympic gold, but with years of training ahead of her, that one big goal was a long way off. When a goal seems a million miles from where you are, maintaining the motivation to keep moving towards it becomes increasing difficult, especially when facing years of hard graft, setbacks, and disappointments. This is where smaller, more manageable steppingstone goals come in, and each one of those goals needs to be a smart goal.

Specific:

Let's say it's your goal to travel the world. What does that mean, exactly? Does it mean visiting every continent; every country in the world; every capital city, or some other goal? Specify. Tell yourself what it is you want to do. (And when we get to 'Recorded', write it down).

Measurable:

Until your goal of travelling the world is made more specific, it's not possible to know when you've achieved it. A specific goal such as visiting every continent can be measured.

Achievable:

A goal needs to be achievable, therefore realistic. Setting yourself the goal of visiting every capital city in the world within the next year is unrealistic if you work full-time and have no savings.

Recorded:

Without records, it's impossible to track progress – or lack of it. Staying on track and maintaining motivation becomes easier when every step along the journey is recorded, and every goal written down.

Time-phased:

Setting daily, weekly, monthly, or yearly targets is an effective way to keep yourself motivated and on track to achieving your goal. Without specific timings, a goal may remain just a dream for another day.

Goals give you direction in life, and making them smart goals gives you clear directions that will take you to your chosen destination. Another method of keeping goals motivational is to make them smart-er goals, which you do by adding exciting and reviewed:

Exciting:

Unless a goal excites you, you're unlikely to stay the course to achieving it. Unless a goal is something you feel passionate about achieving, you're unlikely to remain motivated to push through any obstacles that block your path along the way.

Reviewed:

When a goal is a long way off, stepping stone goals help to keep you on track to achieving it. Each smaller goal successfully achieved gives your motivation a boost, helping to keep you progressing towards the big goal. However, reviewing your goals at timely intervals can help you to consider whether you're still motivated by them. A goal you've held for a long time may no longer be something you feel passionate about achieving, and your interests may have changed. Reviewing and re-evaluating each goal can help to renew your passion OR set you on a path to achieving a new goal that relights your fire. As journalist Kathy Seligman once said, *"You can't hit a home run unless you step up to the plate. You can't catch a fish unless you put your line in the water. You can't reach your goals if you don't try."* A goal that remains something you feel passionate about achieving is a goal that you are mentally and physically prepared to work towards, no matter how long it takes.

Thinking positively and using positive language allows positive changes to be made and positive steps taken. With a positive mental attitude, the way you feel and the actions you take become positively charged, and those positive actions bring positive outcomes in return. As James Allen, author of *'As a Man Thinketh'* once said, *"Work joyfully and peacefully, knowing that right thoughts and right efforts will inevitably bring about right results."*

Chapter 10

The Power of Words

In the story of 'The Little Engine That Could', the words 'I can' helped him to do what the other engines couldn't. The little engine thought he could do it, he believed he could do it, and by saying 'I can' out loud, he put all of the positive energy being created in his thoughts into action – and he did it. This is a great example of positive self-talk.

Self-talk is your internal dialogue; it's the words you're hearing inside your head as you talk out your thoughts for no one other than yourself to hear. The quality of your self-talk depends on you. Positive people have positive self-talk; negative people have negative self-talk. Either way, the inner voice you hear reveals your thoughts, beliefs, questions, and ideas.

The things your inner voice tells you are often things you were told as a child. Parents, teachers, siblings, or other family members may have put negative beliefs about yourself into your mind with scolding words such as, "You can't do anything right... You'll never amount to anything... You never learn..." As the years pass, the negativity is stored away and replayed over and over in your mind whenever you make a mistake, fuelling feelings of hopelessness, anger, guilt, or fear each time you face a difficulty. The amazing thing is that just by swapping positive alternatives for the negative language of your self-talk, you can completely change the way you feel and the way you respond to difficult situations.

An example of negative self-talk might be: *"I really messed up at work today; I made a total mess of it. I'll probably get fired. I can't do anything right. How can I have even let that happen? No wonder I can't get a promotion."*

An alternative example using positive self-talk might be: *"I messed up at work today, but I learned something from it. I see where I went wrong, and I know what I can do to do a much better job next time. I've still got a handle on this, and I can still get that promotion."*

The way you talk to yourself and the words you use set the tone for the way you feel and the way you behave. Negativity can only ever keep you stuck in a downward spiral, but changing negative language for positive is all it takes to give yourself the lift you need to move on. Just as thinking positively is *not* wearing rose-tinted glasses, positive self-talk is *not* self-deception, it's recognising the truth – not just in the situation, but also in yourself. Expecting to go through life without ever making a mistake is unrealistic, and expecting perfection in everything you do and all that you are is equally so. Things won't always go your way and unwanted things will still happen, but when you choose to drown out negative self-talk with positive self-talk you give yourself the opportunity to grow from the experience, learn, and become a better person. For example, you might tell yourself, "I have learned from my mistake, and I will use it to grow. As I grow, I am becoming a better person." When mistakes happen, positive self-talk helps to find the positives that can always be found in seemingly negative events, and that helps you to do better, do more, or simply keep moving forward. This is why learning to recognise the voices in your head and choosing to replace negative voices with positive *can* change your life.

> *"You will find that, just in proportion as you increase your confidence in yourself by the affirmation of what you are determined to be and to do, your ability will increase. No matter what other people may think or say about you, never allow yourself to doubt that you can do what you will to do."*
> – Orison Swett Marden

Numerous studies of self-talk's benefits have shown that positive self-talk can be an effective way to manage stress and enhance your overall well-being, but other interesting possible benefits include: a healthier immune system; improved mental health; better cardiovascular health; increased vitality; reduced pain; reduced stress; greater life satisfaction; and even an increased lifespan. The exact reasons for these potential benefits are unclear, but it's evident that having a positive outlook helps to reduce stress and therefore limits the detrimental effects it can have on physical and mental health. It's possible that there's a general connection between positive thinking and living a healthier lifestyle which would help to promote many of the listed benefits – the healthy body, healthy mind connection.

Hidden Messages

Japanese researcher Masaru Emoto believes that words and thoughts have power to both heal and harm. His research is centred on water, and his discovery that frozen crystals formed in water from clear springs show brilliant, colourful, and complex snowflake patterns, in contrast to those formed in polluted water which show incomplete patterns and only dull colours. This led Masaru to explore further, and his findings were amazing. He found that water exposed to loving, kind thoughts and corresponding words formed beautiful, colourful crystals like those found in spring water, and water exposed to negative thoughts such as anger and hatred formed dull, asymmetric crystals like those found in polluted water. Masaru proposes that, since water has the ability to receive a wide range of frequencies, it can also reflect the universe in this way. When you consider that our bodies are 70 per cent water and the planet we live on is 70 per cent water, this discovery has profound significance. As a result of his research, he believes that we can heal ourselves and our planet by consciously expressing love and goodwill in our thoughts and words.

"What you know is possible in your heart is possible."
– Masaru Emoto

Brené Brown is a research professor who has spent decades studying courage, vulnerability, shame, and empathy. It's her belief that many of us slip into negative self-talk and putting ourselves down because we're trying to live up to unrealistic expectations – such as never making a mistake – or we're trying to be the person society says we should be, rather than accepting ourselves as who we are and following our hearts to become the best we can be. Trying to be 'perfect' in every way and beating yourself up when you make a mistake can only keep you in a negative frame of mind, and only negative energy can be returned to you. Hearing the inner voice, acknowledging the words, and then shutting down negative dialogues with positive alternatives is a powerful way to turn self-talk from a destructive inner conversation into a motivational tool. However, it's also important *not* to let the existence of negative self-talk lead to feelings of failure over your inability to silence the voices. Remember, no one is positive *all* the time, and a bad day is just that – a day. A day where it feels like everything is going wrong doesn't make *you* wrong. A day where you've failed to meet a target doesn't make *you* a failure, and a day where you've given in to the negativity of your inner voice and chosen to wallow in self-pity doesn't mean you can't take back control and turn things around tomorrow. Your attitude or your mood is always your choice, and you can always take back control, no matter how persuasive the negative voice of self-doubt may be.

"Talk to yourself like you would to someone you love."
– Brené Brown

You already know that misery likes company, so it's no surprise that you're more likely to use negative language when you're talking to yourself on a day when you're feeling low. If you're questioning why things never work out for you, or why you're such an idiot, or why you can't be like other people who don't mess up like you do, you're going to find no shortage of negativity in the self-talk answers that come back to you. The lower your mood, the more convincing the negative voice becomes, and the more likely you are to believe every word it says. To break the downward cycle, try imagining how you'd respond to a friend who told you that they felt they were a walking disaster area – would you wholeheartedly agree and give them lots more reasons to back up their belief? No. You would turn their attention to all the reasons why they should believe the opposite; you would remind them of all the positive traits they have and all the good things they have going on in life. This is why you should talk to yourself like you would to someone you love.

When all you're hearing in your mind is negative self-talk, you need to act to turn things around before the negative cycle spirals downwards into a place it's hard to escape from. Ways of breaking free include:

Meeting with friends – talking to someone about the way you're feeling isn't always easy. Saying what's on your mind can make you feel like you're dragging others down, so the tendency is to pretend everything's okay, or avoid socialising completely. Neither option will change the voices in your head because there are no voices of reason to challenge the negativity. Pretending everything is okay is lying to yourself as well as others, and it only creates more negative energy in your world.

Talking to a friend who knows you is an opportunity to talk your thoughts out loud, and sometimes just hearing the words outside your mind can be enough to weaken their hold on you as you begin to question the truth in them. A friend who loves you will listen, and then they'll be that voice of reason. 'A problem shared is a problem halved' is a wise old adage, and getting something off your chest can be the lift you need to start answering the voices of negativity in your mind with your own positive alternatives.

Be okay with not being okay – turning things around is the goal, but until you accept that you're not okay, you can't take steps to make changes for the better. Part of the acceptance process is going to mean allowing yourself to cry, or feel angry, or disappointed... or whatever negative emotion is weighing heavily on you. When you do that, you're being honest with yourself. Pretending you're not upset or giving yourself a hard time over being upset can only create more negative energy that will keep you stuck. Be honest with yourself about your situation and the way you're feeling. When you face up to the reality, you put yourself in a place to begin challenging the negativity.

Do something you love – the key word here is *do*. When negative self-talk is ruling your mind, *doing* something positive can give you a mental as well as a physical lift. Getting outside and going for a walk in nature is a great way to remind yourself of everything that's good in the world, and doing any activity that makes you smile is a positive way to begin turning your self-talk around.

Journal your thoughts – in the same way that talking through your thoughts out loud with a friend can help you to gain a whole new perspective, writing down your thoughts in a journal can be equally beneficial. Writing about the events in your daily life and the way you're feeling about them can help you to identify the things that bring joy into your life, the negative patterns of behaviour that may be repeating, and the language you're using in your self-talk when things are or are not going your way. If you don't recognise negative words when they start to dominate your inner conversations, you won't get that essential early prompt to take action. Just as speaking out loud can lead you to ask whether what you're saying is really true, so can seeing your thoughts written out in front of you. Taking time out to journal every day gives you an opportunity to be absolutely honest with yourself and to sort through the 'noise' in your mind. It can help you to see things differently: are things *really* as bad as your inner voice is telling you? Is it really true that *nothing* ever goes your way? Looking back through the pages of a journal can serve as a powerful reminder of things in your life to feel positive about and be grateful for.

Negative self-talk has a way of drowning out any positivity in your mind, so recognising it is a crucial step to being able to *change* it. This brings us back to the need to know yourself, and to be true to yourself in all you think and all you do. Self-talk doesn't always make sense, and it doesn't need to have the last word; you can choose to change the dialogue. Recognising when you're unhappy gives you the prompt you need to make changes, and recognising when you're trying to be someone or something you're not gives you the understanding you need to change your life for the better. Brené Brown is a great believer in being true to yourself. She says, *"Authenticity is the daily practice of letting go of who we think we're supposed to be and embracing who we are... When we deny our stories, they define us. When we own our stories, we get to write the ending."*

Recognising Negative Thinking

Sometimes negative thinking can become a habit that's accepted as 'normal' in your life and therefore not something you're actively seeking to change. For as long as negativity rules your thoughts, the positive things you want in life are being repelled. Take a moment to consider the negative thinking processes outlined below and see if any of them resonate with you. And be honest when you do this!

Magnifying – you always focus on the downsides of things, overlooking all the upsides. For example, you might go on a day trip to a new city, and then all you have to say about it afterwards revolves around the difficulties you encountered on your journey, not the amazing sights you saw.

Polarising – you see things as either good or bad, black or white, and there's no middle ground. Do this and anything less than perfection will seem like total failure.

Catastrophising – you always expect the worst. You make mountains out of molehills. For example, you spill your coffee on your shirt at breakfast and then adopt an attitude of *everything* going wrong from that point forward and expect your whole day to be a disaster. Be in no doubt: if you think that's what will happen, it will.

Personalising – you blame yourself whenever something bad happens. For example, one of your work colleagues is in a really bad mood and you automatically assume it must be because of something you've done.

Recognising the way you're thinking is an important step towards *changing* the way you're thinking. You can't find a solution to a problem you haven't acknowledged exists. When the voices in your head are negative, it's time to challenge what you're telling yourself and replace negative self-talk with positive self-talk. Instead of magnifying and keeping your focus on how much you hate the hassle of travelling, choose to turn your thoughts to the amazing travel experiences you've had and the wonders of the places you've visited. Instead of polarising and thinking that anything less than perfect makes you a failure, choose to think in terms of good enough, and build from there. Good enough *can* become better, and maintaining a positive attitude helps bring into your life the people and things you need to do better. Instead of catastrophising and making mountains out of molehills, accept unwanted happenings for what they are, just happenings in a moment of time, not happenings that set the tone for the rest of the day – unless you *choose* to adopt and maintain a negative mindset. Instead of personalising, turn your self-talk around by talking to yourself in the same way you would a friend who was choosing to give themselves a hard time over something that's not their doing. Positive self-talk is about changing the script, and choosing to focus on self-acceptance rather than self-judgement.

You can make positive thinking the norm by making it part of your daily routine. Start in the morning by standing in front of a mirror and saying a few positive affirmations that are meaningful to you. In the sales example used previously, this might be, "Today is a good day, I'm going to make a lot of sales," but to be effective, the statements you use must hold special meaning that's specific to you. For example, "I believe in myself; I am strong; I have all I need to be my best; I am enough..." Listen to uplifting music or inspirational podcasts as you go through your morning routine, whether that's on your commute into work or during your breaks. Use post-it notes around your office or in the places you spend most time during your day, writing on them your own motivational words or inspirational quotes that resonate with you. During your lunch break, read an uplifting book, listen to feelgood music, go for a stroll around a nearby park, or meet with upbeat friends, ensuring you surround yourself with positivity wherever possible. Then, in the evening or at the end of your day, take some quiet time to write your thoughts in a journal, and jot down three things that made you smile or three things you feel grateful for that day.

Establishing positive thinking habits will help to change your energy, and the positivity you send out through your thoughts and self-talk will be returned to you.

However, do not expect to feel positive about everything all of the time. That is simply unrealistic. Negativity will creep back into your thoughts and self-talk from time to time, but you can choose not to listen, or you can choose to question what you're hearing. Is there any real evidence to back up the negative statements?

The words and tone of voice you use when you're talking to yourself will be reflected in the way you see yourself and the world you live in. A powerful example of this was found in a 2013 study of anorexic women. Scientists studied the women's movement as they walked through a series of doorways, and it was noted that they would turn themselves sideways to step through doors when there was ample room to walk through facing forwards. They believed themselves to be too fat to fit through, and their self-talk fed them a constant stream of negative comments to back up their beliefs. Whether the voice in your head is telling you facts or fiction, the power of the words you hear and choose to believe can shape your entire perception of who you are and what you're capable of.

Keeping it Real

Staying in the present is also a powerful way to take back control of your thoughts when negativity creeps in. Keep your focus on what's happening in the here and now and you limit the potential to get caught up in worries over events that have already happened or have yet to happen. Past happenings can no longer be changed, but you *can* influence what happens in the present, and therefore what happens in the future.

It takes practice to stay in the present, but simple ways to give yourself reminders throughout the day include:

- Paying attention to the aromas that help you wake up in the morning, whether it's your favourite shower gel or the smell of coffee brewing. Take time to notice them and how they make you feel.
- Paying attention to the environment around you when you're outside, and noticing every effect it has on each of your senses.
- And when you're with friends and loved ones, *really* listening to what they're saying and actively letting them know you're paying attention.

The way you talk to yourself in your thoughts can be the difference between success or failure in life. Positive self-talk can change your attitude and your view of the world, and changing your thoughts influences the actions you take and thereby your outcomes. A positive attitude can help you get through whatever obstacles you face on your journey to becoming the best you can be, whereas a negative attitude will stop you in your tracks at the first hurdle.

Staying in the present and having a heart-to-heart talk with yourself when you find your mind fixating on past or future worries is a great way to sort through your thoughts, and then question the voices in your mind. Talking your thoughts out loud can also help to shed light on what's fact and what's fiction, and get to the root of what's holding you back and preventing you from achieving the life you want. As part of your daily journaling, write out a list of your strengths and weaknesses, paying attention to the qualities and character traits you believe you have and those you want to have. Setting things out in writing can be a great reminder of the positive qualities you have, qualities that may have been overshadowed by doubts and fears, and a means of identifying the qualities you admire in others. Use characteristics such as enthusiasm, strength, patience, cheerfulness, ambition, optimism, perseverance, concentration, and thoroughness. Which do you rate highly in others, and which would you like to develop in yourself. Knowing what it is you want and why you want it sets you on a path to finding it.

Changing Habits

Successful people have successful habits, and these may include living in the present and paying attention to the language they're using in their self-talk. If you recognise that you need to change your habits, remember that people say it takes 21 days to establish a new habit. But three weeks may not be enough – other studies have concluded that establishing a new pattern of behaviour, whether it's in the way you think or in the way you behave, takes closer to 60 days. You already know that, if you want things to be different, you must do things differently, and establishing a new way of thinking or doing is going to take committed effort. This is where goal setting and journaling can help you. Set yourself a time period of at least 60 days and then mark your journal with daily or weekly goals that are going to take you one step at a time towards your new habit being easier to do than not to do – it's habit.

Even those we perceive to have 'made it' and who we assume will already have firmly established successful habits may find themselves falling victim to negative self-talk from time to time, especially if they allow the pressures of being in the public eye to raise doubts over their worthiness. Positive self-talk can be used by anyone, and here are a few examples of positive affirmations used by famous and successful women:

"You are fearless. You're not scared of anything."
– Selena Gomez, singer, actress, and producer

*"You are bold. You are brilliant,
and you are beautiful."*
– Ashley Graham, plus size model and TV presenter

"There are no mistakes, only opportunities."
– Tina Fey, actress, comedian, writer,
producer, and playwright

"No one can tell you who you are except for you."
– Serena Williams, tennis champion

And the last word on this topic goes to producer, screenwriter, and author Shonda Rhimes:
"You have a right to the universe. You are given that right simply by being born."

Final Thoughts and the Very Last word

The golden thread linking the contents of this book is that achieving what you want in life begins and ends with believing in yourself as the person you are, and remaining true to the person you believe yourself to be as you become your best self. Throughout history and across all walks of life, this message has been shared through many teachings and words of wisdom...

"Believe in yourself and have faith in your abilities!
Without humble but reasonable confidence in your
own powers, you cannot be successful or happy."
– Norman Vincent Peale

"To find yourself, think for yourself."
– Socrates

"Trust yourself. Create the kind of self that
you'll be happy to live with all your life.
Make the most of yourself by fanning the tiny,
inner sparks of possibility into
flames of achievement." – Golda Meir

"Always be a first-rate version of yourself and
not a second-rate version of
someone else." – Judy Garland

"Tension is who you think you should be, relaxation
is who you are." – Chinese proverb

"Honesty and transparency make you vulnerable.
Be honest and transparent anyway."
– Mother Theresa

"Listen to your inner voice for it is a deep and powerful
source of wisdom, beauty, and truth, ever flowing
through you." – Caroline Joy Adams

And the final words in this book are to remind you that you, as a young woman, may find yourself at times feeling lost in life like the lion cub in the old fable. The lost lion cub then believes himself to be a sheep, doing what all the other sheep around him do, until the roar of a lion in the distance awakens the sleeping lion within him – his true, magnificent self. Remember, you are not a sheep; you can listen to your inner voice and follow any path in life you choose, and you already have all the resources you need within you to become the best you can be, and to live an abundant life of joy, fulfilment, and true success.

The End

Other Books By
Robert N. Jacobs

Daily Reflections: 365 Days of Contemplation for Mind & Soul.
ISBN: 9781803811642

Aspire for Abundance. Conversations With My Teenage Daughter. Road Trip Through Iceland.
ISBN: 9781803810218